Historical American Biographies

WILLIAM SEWARD

The Mastermind of the Alaska Purchase

Zachary Kent

Enslow Publishers, Inc.

40 Industrial Road   PO Box 38
Box 398   Aldershot
Berkeley Heights, NJ 07922 Hants GU12 6BP
USA   UK

http://www.enslow.com

Library of Congress Cataloging-in-Publication Data

Kent, Zachary.
    William Seward : the mastermind of the Alaska Purchase / Zachary
Kent.
        p. cm. — (Historical American biographies)
    Includes bibliographical references and index.
    ISBN 0-7660-1391-X
    1. Seward, William Henry, 1801–1872—Juvenile literature. 2. Cabinet
officers—United States—Biography—Juvenile literature. 3. Statesmen—
United States—Biography—Juvenile literature. 4. Alaska—Annexation
to the United States—Juvenile literature. 5. United States—Foreign
relations—1861–1865—Juvenile literature. 6. United States—Politics and
government—1861–1865—Juvenile literature. [1. Seward, William
Henry, 1801–1872. 2. Statesmen. 3. United States—Politics and
government—1861–1865. 4. Alaska—Annexation to the United States.]
    I. Title. II. Series.
    E415.9.S4 K46 2001
    973.7'092—dc21
                                            00-009427

Printed in the United States of America

10 9 8 7 6 5 4 3 2 1

To Our Readers: All Internet addresses in this book were active and appropriate
at the time we went to press. Any comments or suggestions can be sent by e-mail
to Comments@enslow.com or to the address on the back cover.

Illustration Credits: Enslow Publishers, Inc., pp. 20, 38, 101; Library of
Congress, pp. 7, 9, 13, 19, 28, 50, 54, 59, 70, 97, 102, 113; National
Archives, pp. 26, 39, 41, 60, 77, 90, 91, 94; Seward House, Auburn,
New York, pp. 17, 31; Zachary Kent, p. 107.

Cover Illustrations: National Archives (Inset); © Corel Corporation
(Background).

CONTENTS

1

SEWARD'S FOLLY

"CASH! CASH! CASH!—Cash paid for cast-off territory," blared mocking headlines in the *New York Herald*.[1] In the spring of 1867, Americans were in an uproar about the purchase of Alaska.

Since the 1740s, Russian fur traders from the Russian-American Company had hunted seal, otter, and fox in the region that is today Alaska. By the autumn of 1866, however, the Russian government needed money. It decided to offer its vast North American territory for sale. The Russian ambassador to the United States, Edouard de Stoeckl, was instructed to make the bargain.

American Secretary of State William Seward certainly wanted to buy. Russian America covered some

591,000 square miles, more than twice the size of Texas. Seward had long desired to add that land to the United States. In an 1860 speech, Seward had remarked,

> Standing here and looking far off into the Northwest, I see the Russian as he busily occupies himself in establishing seaports and towns . . . and I . . . say, "Go on, and build up your outposts all along the coast, even up to the Arctic Ocean—they will yet become the outposts of my own country."[2]

In March 1867, President Andrew Johnson gave Seward permission to begin negotiations. For several days, Seward and Stoeckl bargained and finally reached an agreement. The United States would pay $7.2 million for the territory—about two cents per acre.

Making a Treaty

On the evening of March 29, 1867, Seward sat at home in Washington, D.C. He was playing cards with friends when the Russian ambassador arrived with good news. The terms for the sale of the territory had been approved by his government. He was prepared to sign the treaty the following day. Seward, with a smile, quickly rose from the card table. He was determined to seize this great opportunity.

"Why wait till to-morrow, Mr. Stoeckl?" he declared. "Let us make the treaty to-night."

"But your department is closed," replied the Russian diplomat. "You have no clerks, and my secretaries are scattered about town."

"Never mind that," answered Seward cheerfully, "if you can [gather your secretaries] together before midnight, you will find me awaiting you at the department, which will be open and ready for business."[3]

Through the early hours of March 30, 1867, Seward, Stoeckl, and their assistants labored at the State Department. As dawn approached, they signed and sealed the treaty documents. Later that day, Seward climbed the steps of the Capitol to urge immediate Senate approval of the treaty. Charles Sumner, chairman of the Senate Foreign Relations

The treaty for the purchase of Alaska was written during the early morning hours of March 30, 1867. In this painting, Secretary of State William Seward sits with a map on his lap, while Russian ambassador Edouard de Stoeckl stands pointing to Alaska on the globe.

Committee, however, insisted that the document first be studied carefully by his committee. In the meantime, startled Americans learned of Seward's bargain.

Public Reaction

Many Americans had no faith in the purchase. They believed that Russian America was a useless, frozen region whose chief products were polar bears and icebergs. Newspaper articles soon mocked the purchase as "Seward's Folly" and called the territory "Seward's Icebox" and "Walrussia."

"Russian America is a dreary waste of snow and ice," exclaimed the Chicago *Evening Journal*.[4] The New York *World* insisted, "Russia has sold us a sucked orange. . . . The Russian possessions . . . are of little immediate value."[5] The New York *Daily Tribune* declared,

> We simply obtain by the treaty . . . deserts of snow, vast tracts of dwarf timbers, [and] frozen rivers. . . . Ninety-nine hundredths of Russian America are absolutely useless; the remaining hundredth may be of some value to the Russians who settled it, but it certainly is not worth seven millions of dollars.[6]

Selling the Idea

To gain support for the treaty, Seward invited senators to dinner parties at his home. While the senators enjoyed fine food and wine, Seward described how beautiful Russian America was reported to be. The *New York Herald*, in an article entitled "Mr. Seward's Dinner Diplomacy," said, "Mr. Seward's dinner table is spread first with a map of Russian America, and this

"THE BIG THING."

OLD MOTHER SEWARD. "I'll rub some of this on his sore spot: it may soothe him a little."

Many Americans believed the purchase of Alaska would be a waste of money. In this newspaper cartoon drawn by artist Thomas Nast, Old Mother Seward rubs a soothing Russian salve on the head of a cranky Uncle Sam.

cloth is covered with roast treaty, boiled treaty, treaty in bottles . . . treaty clad in furs, ornamented with walrus teeth, fringed with timber and flopping with fish."[7]

Some people, however, thought Seward was right. The Boston *Herald* declared of the purchase,

> . . . those who know most about it, estimate it most highly. . . . The country is reported to abound in furs, forest, and minerals, while [the] rivers and bays on its coast swarm with as fine fish as ever were caught. . . . As to the price, there can be but one opinion—it is dog cheap.[8]

In time, the Senate Foreign Relations Committee reached its decision. Senator Sumner rose in the Senate chamber and delivered a long speech recommending approval of the treaty. After much discussion, on April 9, 1867, the Senate approved the treaty by a vote of 37 to 2. Seward's admirers suggested that the territory be called "Seward Land" or "Seward Territory." "Aliaska," "Yukon," and "Sitka" were other names suggested. At Senator Sumner's suggestion, though, the name "Alaska," from an Aleut (Alaskan native) word meaning mainland, was chosen for the territory.[9]

The House of Representatives decided to delay the vote for money to pay for Alaska. With the purchase again in danger, Seward swung into action. With personal charm and intelligent arguments, he persuaded key congressmen how valuable Alaska would be to the United States. On July 14, 1868, the House finally voted the necessary funds to buy the territory.

After Seward retired from office in 1869, one of his neighbors asked him what his greatest success had been as secretary of state. Seward replied without hesitation that it had been the Alaska Purchase. "But," he added, "it will take the country a generation to appreciate it."[10]

Almost single-handedly, William Seward had made Alaska part of the United States. The buying of Alaska marked the end of Seward's remarkable career in public service. As governor of New York, as a United States senator, and as United States secretary of state during the Civil War, William Seward was one of the true political giants of nineteenth-century America.

2

THE LAWYER
FROM
AUBURN

I was the fourth of six children, and the third son,"
William Henry Seward later recalled.[1] He was born
on May 16, 1801, in the village of Florida, New York,
about sixty miles north of New York City. His father,
Dr. Samuel Seward, was one of Florida's leading citizens. Not only did Dr. Seward practice medicine, but he
was also a successful merchant, a wealthy landowner,
and a local politician. His mother, Mary Jennings
Seward, was a kind, warm-hearted woman. She was a
"person of excellent sense, gentleness, [and] truthful-
ness," Seward remembered.[2]

The new baby in the Seward household was given
the nickname Harry. He grew into a bright but sickly
child. "My health caused me to be early set apart," he
later admitted.[3] Harry Seward's first education was in

Florida's one-room schoolhouse. Then, for a while, he attended Farmer's Hall Academy, six miles away in the town of Goshen. But soon he returned to Florida, where he hiked each day to the new Florida Academy. He spent long hours studying reading, writing, and arithmetic.

On the Seward farm he also did daily chores. "It was my business," he later described, "to drive the cows, morning and evening, to and from distant pastures, to chop and carry [wood] for the parlor-fire . . . and to do the errands of the family generally."[4]

Although Dr. Seward lived in the North, he owned several slaves. Landowners in southern New York

Given the nickname "Harry," William Henry Seward grew up on the family farm in Florida, New York.

often used slave labor on their farms. Slavery would not be outlawed in New York until 1827. Harry Seward often sat in the kitchen listening to the family's slaves tell stories. "The tenants of the kitchen," he fondly remembered, ". . . had a fund of knowledge about the ways and habits of the devil, of witches, of ghosts, and of men who had been hanged."[5] Young Seward treated the slaves as his friends, and he helped the slave children learn how to read.

The College Student

In 1816, Dr. Seward sent his fifteen-year-old son off to Union College, in Schenectady, New York. Of all the Seward children, Dr. Seward decided that Harry would be the one to get a college education. The intelligent teenager qualified to enter the junior class, but because of his age, he was enrolled in the sophomore class.

Seward looked younger than fifteen. Thin and pale, he never grew taller than five feet five inches in height. Classmates often teased him about his thick red hair and made jokes about his simple, country-style clothing. His feelings hurt, he finally visited a Schenectady tailor and bought expensive new clothes. He hoped his father would pay the bills, but when Dr. Seward received them, he angrily refused. He believed his son was wasting hard-earned money.

Running Away From Home

His father's treatment greatly upset Seward. On New Year's Day, 1819, the eighteen-year-old boy ran away

from college. He joined a classmate who had been offered a teaching position in Georgia. The two traveled by stagecoach to New York City, then boarded a ship bound for Savannah, Georgia.

When they reached Georgia, Seward's friend decided to accept a different teaching job. Seward realized his wallet was nearly empty. He applied for the teaching position his friend had turned down. Soon after, Union Academy in Eatonville, Georgia, advertised that Mr. William H. Seward, "late from Union College, New York," would be teaching "the Latin and Greek languages. . . . Mathematics, Logic, Rhetoric . . . Philosophy, Chemistry, Geography, [and] English grammar."[6] His salary would be one hundred dollars a year. That was enough for a person to live on in 1819.

Within weeks, Seward's parents discovered where he had gone. Before long, sad letters arrived from his mother, urging him to come home. The young teacher finally agreed and returned north in June 1819. That summer, he studied law in Goshen, and in the fall, returned to Union College. His hard work at school earned him an invitation to join the respected academic honor society Phi Beta Kappa. In July 1820, nineteen-year-old William Seward graduated from college with high honors.

After his graduation, Seward continued his legal training. He studied first with Goshen lawyer John Duer and then in the New York City office of John Anthon. His long hours studying legal books paid off when he took the bar examination in Utica, New

York, in October 1822. He answered only one question incorrectly.

The Attraction of Auburn

Traveling home from Utica, Seward stopped in Auburn, New York. There, he visited Frances Miller, a young woman who had attended private school with Seward's sister, Cornelia. People who met Seward thought him an ambitious young man, full of energy, friendly, and outgoing. Seward thought eighteen-year-old Frances Miller was attractive, charming, and intelligent. He liked her very much.

During his Auburn visit, two law firms offered Seward positions as a junior partner. He agreed to join the office of Frances Miller's father, Judge Elijah Miller. It was a good job, and it would allow him to stay near Frances. In December 1822, he moved to Auburn.

Seward took up his new law duties with energy and continued to court Frances Miller. In the summer of 1823, she accepted his proposal of marriage. They traveled by horse-drawn carriage during an engagement trip to Niagara Falls. While driving through the muddy streets of Rochester, New York, their carriage lost a wheel. A tall, sturdy, young newspaper editor named Thurlow Weed stepped forward and helped Seward remount the wheel. The two men instantly liked one another. Their chance meeting that day marked the start of an important friendship. In future years, Weed would become Seward's most valued political supporter.

On October 20, 1824, William Henry Seward and Frances Miller exchanged marriage vows in St. Paul's Episcopal Church in Auburn. Judge Miller, a widower, could not bear to have his daughter live apart from him. He insisted that the newlyweds move into his house on South Street. It was a large, brick house surrounded by poplar and apple trees, one of the finest homes in Auburn. While Frances looked after the household, Seward continued his law career.

The Anti-Mason Movement

A social organization called the Freemasons, with secret oaths and handshakes, caused an uproar throughout the United States in 1826. That year, William Morgan

In Auburn, New York, Seward fell in love with Frances Miller, the beautiful daughter of Judge Elijah Miller. These portraits of Seward and his wife were painted a few years after they were married.

published a book revealing some of the society's secrets. Soon after, Morgan disappeared under mysterious circumstances. Many people suspected he had been murdered by angry Masons. Seward soon became caught up in the excitement caused by Morgan's disappearance. In 1828, he joined the new Anti-Mason political movement. The Anti-Masons insisted that the powerful Freemasons should not be allowed to get away with murder.

The Anti-Masons elected Seward to attend their state and national conventions in 1830. Seward's rising interest in politics attracted the notice of Thurlow Weed. Weed now owned a newspaper, the *Evening Journal*, in the state capital of Albany. He urged Seward to run for the New York state senate on the Anti-Mason ticket.

In the autumn campaign, Seward easily won election to a four-year term. At the end of December, he packed his trunks and rode the stagecoach to Albany, a 165-mile trip that took three days. At the Eagle Tavern he found a room to rent. He would live there by himself while Frances remained behind in Auburn to care for their two little sons, Augustus, born in 1826, and Frederick, born in 1830.

State Senator

Seward solemnly took the oath of office on January 4, 1831. At thirty years of age, he became the youngest member of the thirty-two-member New York Senate. Among the other six Anti-Mason members was Thurlow Weed. The two men quickly became close

EAGLE TAVERN,

CORNER OF BROADWAY & HAMILTON ST.,
ALBANY.

We have leased the EAGLE TAVERN for a Term of years, and have cleansed and regenerated it from top to bottom. No exertion on our part shall be wanting to make the "Eagle" what it has been in "days gone by."

ALFRED HOUGHTON.
Late of the Steamboat Knickerbocker.

PETER ACKER,
Late of the Townsend House.

N. B.----A careful Porter will be in attendance to take charge of Baggage.

The new owners of the Eagle Tavern hotel posted this advertisement in Albany. While serving as a New York state senator, Seward lived in a room there.

friends. Seward enjoyed Weed's visits to his room. "He sits down," he described, "stretches one of his long legs out to rest on my coal-box; I cross my own; and, puffing the smoke of our cigars into each other's faces, we talk of everything and everybody."[7] Weed loved politics and making political deals. As his influence grew in New York, Weed was given the nickname "The Dictator." Seward wrote to his wife, "Weed is the only man whose entire confidence I have or who has mine."[8]

As a state senator, Seward remained in Albany four months out of each year. During his first term, he

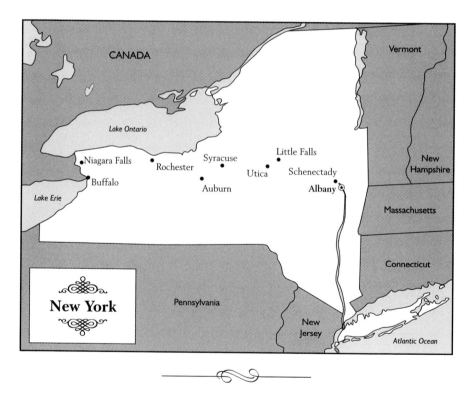

This map of New York shows some of the cities associated with Seward's youth and early career.

supported a law abolishing imprisonment for debt and also presented a bill to establish a separate state prison for women. In addition, he supported the building of railroads and canals, because he firmly believed in improving methods of transportation in New York.

A Trip to Europe

For many years, Dr. Seward had longed to visit Europe. In 1833, he invited his son to make the journey with him and offered to pay all the expenses. Dr. Seward was an old man now, and he needed a traveling companion. Seward happily agreed to go with his father. He also promised to write a series of letters about his travels that Weed could publish in the Albany *Evening Journal.*

The father and son sailed from New York City on June 1, 1833, aboard the ship *Europe.* The ship plowed across the Atlantic waves and reached Liverpool, England, in eighteen days. They visited London first and then traveled to Ireland and Scotland. Then, they crossed the English Channel and toured Holland and Germany. In Switzerland, Seward climbed the heights of Mont Blanc. Full of excitement and energy, he often rose early so he could set out ahead of the stagecoach. He ended up walking half the distance from Geneva, Switzerland, to Paris, France. In Paris, Seward and his father gazed at impressive paintings at the Louvre Museum and strolled through the beautiful Tuileries Gardens. They also met the great Revolutionary War hero, the Marquis de Lafayette.

Seward sent the letters he promised to Thurlow Weed. As many as seventy of them eventually appeared in Weed's newspaper. In November 1833, Seward and his father arrived back in New York. The five-month trip proved very valuable to Seward. Not only did he see the sights but he learned a great deal about Europe's people and politics.

A Race for the Governorship

A new political party called the Whigs sprang into existence in 1834. Anti-Masons, National Republicans, and some Southern Democrats all merged together to oppose the policies of Democratic President Andrew Jackson. Thurlow Weed became the leader of the Whig party in New York. Weed wished to make Seward the Whig candidate for governor that year, and Seward won the nomination. He would challenge Democratic Governor William Marcy.

Seward gave up his seat in the state senate to concentrate on his campaign. During the campaign, the Whigs charged that the New York Democrats were corrupt, calling them the "ruffled shirt party."[9] The Democrats, they claimed, lived in marble palaces and rode in fancy coaches. Elect Seward, the Whigs declared, and he would bring honesty to the state government. The Democrats spread rumors that Seward was only twenty-two years old when he was in fact thirty-three. One Democratic newspaper called him "a man of small abilities [and] little experience."[10]

On election day, Seward did well in western New York. Still, he lost the election by eleven thousand votes. The loss greatly disappointed Seward, but he told a friend, "I have got quite over being beat. . . . Don't let it vex you. We have had glory enough already."[11] Despite his defeat, Seward became the leading figure in New York's Whig party.

A Summer Vacation

Doctors advised Frances Seward to take a vacation for her health. She often complained of headaches and sleeplessness. In May 1835, Seward, his wife, and their five-year-old son, Fred, set off on a carriage tour to Virginia. The carriage rolled along at a rate of twenty miles a day. From his cushioned seat, Seward gazed at the roads, the scenery, and the people they passed. "There is an air of quiet . . . about these villages," Seward happily wrote as they journeyed through Pennsylvania, "which . . . gives them an especial charm. The log-houses in this country are altogether superior to ours. . . . I never could have imagined a log-house so attractive as many I have seen here."[12]

In Virginia, the Sewards witnessed some of the sorrows of slavery. One day, they talked to a slave woman whose husband and six children had all been sold to plantations far away. On another day, they saw a shackled gang of slave boys herded to a horse trough to drink. Seward wrote to his father, "The entire country in Virginia exhibits [the] melancholy evidence of . . . slave labor."[13] Seeing the effects of Southern slavery firsthand made a great impact on him. After visiting Washington, D.C., the Sewards finished their trip and returned to Auburn in September.

The Rise of Horace Greeley

A young journalist named Horace Greeley became an ally of Seward and Weed during Seward's 1838 campaign for governor. Greeley edited the Whig newspaper the *Jeffersonian*. In 1841, Greeley founded the *New York Tribune*, which would become one of the most important newspapers in the nation. Among the advice Greeley gave his *Tribune* readers were the famous words, "Go west, young man." Greeley correctly believed that the undeveloped West offered Americans many new economic opportunities.

Another Try for the Governorship

Seward worked hard as a lawyer and also served for a time as a real estate agent, but he never lost his interest in politics. "Keep me informed upon political matters," he wrote to Weed.[14] During 1837 and 1838, Weed crisscrossed New York, promoting Seward as the best possible Whig candidate for governor. When the state convention met in September 1838, Seward won the nomination again. Once more, he would run against William Marcy.

During the 1838 campaign, Weed tirelessly traveled the state gathering support for Seward. "Indications and signs are good," he wrote to Seward as election day neared.[15] When the ballots were finally counted, Seward learned he had won by ten thousand votes. He would be the next governor of New York. "God bless Thurlow Weed!" he exclaimed. "I owe this result to him."[16]

3

GOVERNOR OF NEW YORK AND PRIVATE CITIZEN

⁓

The excitement of the election has ceased. . . . Heavy responsibilities will soon be heaped upon me," thirty-seven-year-old Seward wrote to his mother soon after his election.[1] He left for Albany with his son Augustus on December 21, 1838. Frances, who was pregnant, was unwilling to make the long journey.

Seward spent his first days in Albany looking for a place to live. He finally rented a mansion at the corner of Waterloo and Broad streets. It was a grand house, but its cost each year would be more than twice Seward's $4,000 salary as governor.

On New Year's Day, 1839, a great crowd attended Seward's inauguration. After taking the oath of office, Seward immediately penned a note to his wife: "My

Seward posed for this picture while serving as governor of New York. Governor Seward worked hard to improve the lives of people in his state.

Dear Frances, —We are here. The ceremony is over. A joyous people throng the capitol."[2]

Twelve-year-old Augustus Seward also wrote home: "I was up to the capitol and saw Pa sworn in his office. . . . Pa come [*sic*] home and let about 2 or 3 thousand people in the house and they crowded in so fast that they upset one of the tables."[3] Supporters thronged to the new governor's mansion to celebrate. They gorged themselves on turkeys, hams, cakes, and punch. Servants passed trays of food through the open windows to feed people jammed together in the yard. Throughout the evening, Governor Seward shook hands with well-wishers until his palms and fingers ached.

The Work of Governor

Seward closely consulted his trusted friend Thurlow Weed in reorganizing the state government. Office-seekers bothered the new governor constantly. From morning to evening they packed the hallways to his office. He received so many letters from office-seekers that answering them kept him busy for months.

Each day, Seward usually rose at six o'clock and worked at his desk until noon. Often Thurlow Weed visited at lunchtime. Then Seward would spend his afternoon at his desk or visiting one of the government departments. As governor, Seward proposed widening the Erie Canal and urged the building of three new railroads. To improve prison standards, Seward fired cruel supervisors at Auburn and Sing Sing state prisons. He also organized programs to teach convicts useful

Pictured here is New York political leader Thurlow Weed, who was called "The Dictator." Throughout his life, Seward could always count on Weed for friendship and advice.

skills. He outlawed prison whippings at Auburn, and ordered that meals be improved at both prisons.

In 1839, an incident occurred that brought Governor Seward national attention. In Virginia, three free African-American sailors unsuccessfully tried to help a slave escape aboard a ship bound for New York City. Virginia Governor Thomas Gilmer demanded that the three sailors be returned to Virginia to stand trial. But Seward refused to arrest the men. "There is no law of this State," he declared, "which recognizes slavery, no statute which admits that one man can be the property of another, or that one man can be stolen from another."[4] Many Virginians fumed, but Northern antislavery leaders praised Governor Seward's attitude.

Educating Immigrant Children

In his inaugural address, Seward had encouraged immigration. "We must extend to [foreigners] the right of citizenship," he had declared. "And we should

The Oneida Indians

While Seward was governor, American Indians of the Oneida tribe were forced by the United States government to give up their New York lands and resettle west of the Mississippi River. Seward could not change federal policy, but he did invite Oneida Chief Moses Schuyler to visit him at the governor's mansion. Seward awkwardly told Schuyler "how reluctantly I have consented to the sale of your lands."[5] The Oneida tribe sadly journeyed westward. They resettled on lands in the territory that would eventually become the state of Oklahoma.

[establish] schools in which their children shall enjoy advantages of education equal to our own."[6] In New York City, thousands of immigrant children roamed the streets without a chance to go to school. As governor, Seward unsuccessfully urged that the state help finance religious schools to help these boys and girls. The school issue made Seward a hero among Irish and German Catholics.

A Return to Private Life

Seward served two two-year terms as governor. By 1842, however, he began to worry about money. The personal debts he had run up while governor now totaled about $200,000. As a result, Seward announced that he would not seek a third term. In one of his last letters as governor, Seward wrote to Thurlow Weed,

"My Dear Weed, —The end has come at last. My successor and the new year are here together. . . . My public career is honorably closed."[7]

In January 1843, Seward returned to Auburn. He put a wooden shingle reading "Wm. H. Seward" outside the Exchange Building on Genesee Street. Two junior partners joined Seward in his new law office. He also hired a number of young law students to serve as clerks. Law clerk James Cox later recalled,

> Constantly interrupted during the day by the visits of . . . friends and village politicians, [Seward's] most efficient labor was generally done at night. He would come into the office after supper, sit down in his writing-chair, and rapidly throw off [pages of manuscript] which would drop on the floor around him like the leaves of the forest.[8]

Seward worked hard at his profession in order to pay off his debts with honor. "I am wearing out old clothes," he wrote to Weed, "burning tallow-candles, smoking a pipe instead of cigars, economizing fuel, and balancing my cash-book night and morning."[9]

Seward at Home

For relaxation, Seward spent long hours improving his yard and garden. Once, while Frances was visiting friends in Rochester, he gave her a report on his activities:

> You will scarcely recognize the place when you see it. . . . I took Augustus with me and two laborers into the woods, and brought home fifteen fine, thrifty elms . . . I have engaged also fifty evergreens and a few mountain ash trees. We have also set out choice gooseberries and raspberries in large quantities.[10]

Seward's family continued to grow. A son, William Henry, was born in 1839, and a daughter, Frances, called "Fanny," was born in 1844. They joined older brothers Augustus and Frederick to complete the Seward family. The children could often be found running in the yard and playing with the family's many pet cats and dogs.

Seward the Lawyer

The Liberty party was dedicated to the antislavery cause. Several times during the 1840s, politicians asked Seward to run for president as the Liberty party candidate. Seward chose instead to keep busy and

Frances Seward is pictured with her three sons, (from left to right) Frederick, William, and Augustus. Augustus attended the United States Military Academy at West Point, New York, and served in the army during the Mexican War.

earn money with his law practice. The inventors of steam-engines, valves, railroad car wheels, and other items called on Seward to help them protect their manufacturing rights. He soon became a successful patent lawyer. Law clerk Frank Chamberlain recalled, "Going into court he always attracted . . . attention. There was something in his appearance that commanded the highest respect."[11]

Two local murder trials brought Seward national fame in 1846. In 1845, at Auburn prison, prisoner Henry Wyatt, an African American, murdered a fellow convict. After meeting with Wyatt, Seward became convinced he was insane and volunteered to defend him. Seward thought brutal prison whippings had caused Wyatt's madness. At Wyatt's trial in February 1846, prison records and medical testimony supported Seward's belief. The jury in Wyatt's first trial failed to reach a verdict. A second trial ended in conviction, and the judge sentenced Wyatt to hang.

At about the same time, on the night of March 12, 1846, an African American named William Freeman stabbed to death farmer John Van Nest, Van Nest's wife, and two others. Freeman had spent five years in prison, enduring harsh treatment, for stealing a horse. On one occasion, he was beaten with a plank and deafened in one ear. Confused, he blamed Van Nest for his imprisonment and killed him for revenge.

Despite the ugliness of the Van Nest murders, Seward soon announced that he would defend Freeman, too. In Auburn taverns, people muttered threats, and Seward received hateful letters in the mail. Friends

urged him to give up the case, but Seward refused. He wrote to Thurlow Weed, "There is a busy war around me, to drive me from defending and securing a fair trial for the negro Freeman."[12]

On July 10, 1846, the Freeman trial began. Seward called on several doctors to describe Freeman's prison beatings and mental condition. In his summary, Seward quoted an African-American witness who had testified: "[Society] made William Freeman what he is, a brute beast; they don't make anything else of our people but brute beasts; but when we violate their laws, then they want to punish us as if we were men."[13]

Despite Seward's efforts, the jury found Freeman guilty and sentenced him to hang. Seward appealed the verdict. After reviewing the case, the state supreme court ordered a new trial. But Freeman died in prison on August 21, 1847, of tuberculosis (a lung disease) before he could come to trial.

Seward had failed to save Freeman, but he had done his best against terrific odds. The effort had been worthwhile. Seward decided that, when he died, the most honorable thing that could be written on his gravestone would be the words "He was Faithful."

The Campaign of 1848

American settlers in the Mexican region called Texas had declared their independence from Mexico in 1836. The Texans won their fight for freedom, and in 1845, Texas joined the United States as the twenty-eighth state. But for years, Texans and Mexicans continued to

argue about their border. In April 1846, cannons roared along the Rio Grande as the Mexican War erupted. At the battles of Palo Alto, Resaca de la Palma, and Monterrey, United States General Zachary Taylor won stunning victories, which eventually helped America win the war against Mexico. Seward soon declared, "General Taylor's last brilliant battles have produced a conviction among Whigs . . . that he will be nominated and elected President."[14] The Whigs supported Taylor even though he owned slaves on his Louisiana plantation.

Taylor received the Whig presidential nomination in 1848. That autumn, Seward campaigned throughout New York, Pennsylvania, Delaware, and Ohio, giving speeches in support of the Whig ticket. The great political issue in the campaign was whether slavery should be allowed in the new territories won from Mexico. In Boston, Massachusetts, Seward addressed an audience at the Tremont Temple. "On the slavery question," he exclaimed, "to this extent all Whigs agree: that slavery shall not be extended into any territory now free."[15] A second speaker followed Seward—a tall, lean Illinois congressman named Abraham Lincoln. Lincoln delivered what Seward later called "a rambling story-telling speech, putting the audience in good humor, but avoiding any extended discussion of the slavery question."[16]

The following night, Seward and Lincoln found themselves sharing the same hotel room. As they prepared for sleep, Lincoln remarked, "I have been thinking about what you said in your speech. I reckon you're right. We have got to deal with this slavery question, and . . . give much more attention to it hereafter than we have been doing."[17]

In November 1848, Whig candidate Zachary Taylor was elected president. Many Whigs also captured seats in the New York state legislature. It was the legislature that would choose the state's newest United States senator. Seward was the leading candidate, and Thurlow Weed campaigned hard on his behalf. On February 6, 1849, the Whig-controlled legislature chose William Seward to go to Washington.

4

ANTISLAVERY SENATOR

"Probably no man ever yet appeared for the first time in Congress so widely known and so warmly appreciated as William H. Seward," declared editor Horace Greeley in the *New York Tribune*.[1] Forty-seven-year-old Seward took his oath as a United States senator on March 5, 1849. He warmly shook hands with his fellow senators and chose a desk in the back row of the Senate chamber.

The Sewards rented a large brick house on F Street in Washington, D.C., for four hundred dollars a year. At first, Frances Seward enjoyed living in the capital. "There are evidences of refinement in the society here," she wrote to her sister, "that I have never found elsewhere."[2] Before long, however, fragile health caused her to return home to Auburn. She took the

children with her. Seward remained behind in Washington to deal with national issues.

A Higher Law

As a result of the Mexican War, the United States gained much western territory. Southern slaveholders wished to extend slavery into these new regions. Southern plantation owners relied on slaves to plant and harvest cotton, rice, tobacco, and other crops. Northerners, on the other hand, had little need for slaves. There, farmers worked small farms themselves, and there were thousands of immigrants to work in Northern factories. Many Northerners resisted the idea of spreading slavery to the West, because additional slave states would give the South greater political power. Many Northerners also regarded slavery as a cruel and immoral institution.

On January 29, 1850, Kentucky Senator Henry Clay rose in the Senate and proposed several important resolutions. He called for the admission of the new California Territory as a free state and the creation of new territorial governments in New Mexico and Utah that might allow slavery if settlers voted for it. Clay also called for a new fugitive slave law to help slave owners reclaim runaway slaves, and the abolition of the slave trade in Washington, D.C. Clay hoped these resolutions, which contained terms favorable to both the North and the South, would bring peace to the nation. They became known as Clay's Compromise, or the Compromise of 1850.

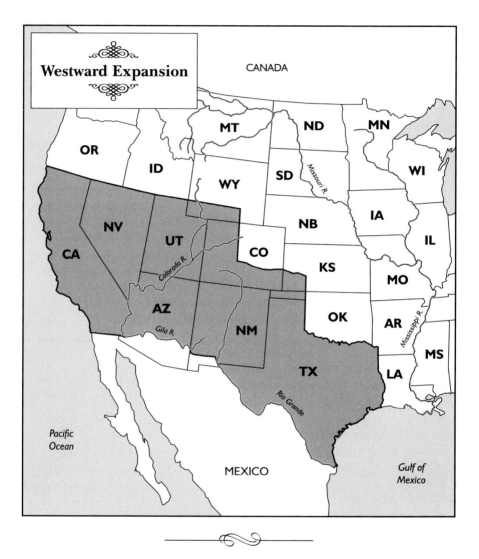

The vast western territories won from Mexico in the 1840s (shaded area) caused the fight over the expansion of slavery to heat up.

Months of debate on the compromise followed. Seward opposed most of Clay's proposals. He called them "magnificent humbug" designed to protect the institution of slavery.[3] On March 11, 1850, he rose in the Senate to respond to Clay. He agreed that California should be admitted as a free state. But he hotly opposed even the possibility of extending slavery into any new American territory. In addition, instead of just stopping the slave trade in Washington, D.C., Seward demanded that slavery be banished completely from the capital. In a hoarse, flat voice he made his plea. He often seemed almost to be talking to himself. But the content of his three-hour speech caught the full attention of his listeners. After attacking Clay's Compromise, he cut to the very heart of the issue. "There is a higher law than the Constitution," he boldly proclaimed. "I feel assured that slavery must give way, and will give way. . . . emancipation is inevitable, and is near."[4]

No senator had ever condemned slavery so openly before. Before

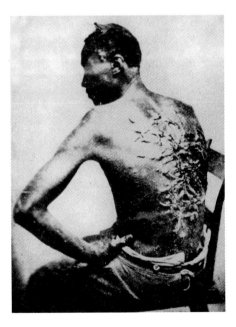

A former slave shows his scarred back, the result of brutal whippings. Slavery in the United States became the great moral issue of the 1850s.

the end of March, one hundred thousand copies of Seward's speech had been printed. It became famous throughout the country as Seward's "Higher Law" speech. "Seward's speech will live longer," declared Horace Greeley, "be read with more hearty admiration, and exert [more] influence on the national mind and character than any other speech of the session."[5] In a single stroke, Seward became the nation's leading antislavery senator.

Death of a President

Throughout the spring and summer of 1850, the Senate continued to debate Clay's Compromise. President Taylor believed California should be admitted as a free state. He seemed to agree with Seward's position regarding the spread of slavery. But Taylor fell ill with severe stomach cramps on July 4, 1850. After sitting in the summer heat, listening to long Independence Day speeches, he had gulped down huge portions of iced milk and cherries. On July 9, Seward wrote home: "I cannot omit to speak my dreadful [fears] about the President. He is in extreme danger."[6] That same day, Taylor died, most likely of cholera, a disease caused by impure water or spoiled food. Vice President Millard Fillmore suddenly became president. Fillmore favored Clay's Compromise. With Fillmore's support, and much assistance from Senator Stephen A. Douglas, the separate parts of the compromise eventually became law.

*Senator William Seward poses with his daughter Fanny. Seward's
antislavery speeches in the Senate earned him the respect of many
Northerners and the hatred of many slaveholding Southerners.*

The North Star

In the midst of the slavery debates of the 1850s, former slave Frederick Douglass edited an antislavery newspaper in Rochester, New York. It was called *The North Star*. (Runaway slaves often followed the north star to freedom in the Northern states and Canada.) William Seward was proud to contribute money to support Douglass's newspaper.

The Kansas-Nebraska Act

During the early 1850s, many Northerners rose up and condemned slavery like never before. At the same time, Southerners looked for ways to spread slavery westward. Both sections feared that the other would expand its political influence by making new territories either slave states or free. On January 23, 1854, Illinois Senator Stephen A. Douglas introduced a bill that would permit slavery into the Kansas-Nebraska territories if voted for by the settlers.

Completely outraged, Seward wrote to his wife: "Douglas has introduced a bill for organizing the Nebraska territory, going as far as the Democrats dare towards abolishing . . . the [1820] Missouri Compromise which devoted all the new regions north of 36° 30' to freedom. I am heart-sick of being here."[7] (The Missouri Compromise had abolished slavery north of the 36° 30' line of latitude in territories of the Louisiana Purchase.)

Seward spoke for three hours in the Senate on the afternoon of February 17, 1854. He declared that a bill had come "bowing, stooping and wriggling into the Senate" that violated both the Missouri Compromise of 1820 and Clay's Compromise of 1850.[8] Despite Seward's protests, Congress passed the Kansas-Nebraska Act in May 1854. President Franklin Pierce, who had been elected in 1852, signed the bill into law.

Antislavery Northerners raged at the new law. In the Senate, Seward exclaimed,

> Come on, then, gentlemen of the slave states! Since there is no escaping your challenge, I accept it in behalf of the cause of freedom. We will engage in competition for the . . . soil of Kansas, and God give the victory to the side which is stronger in number, as it is in the right![9]

Many Northerners quickly voiced their support. From Springfield, Illinois, lawyer William Herndon soon sent Seward a letter. Seward, he remarked, had "a fast and growing popularity out West." He added, "Mr. Lincoln, my partner and your friend . . . thinks your speech most excellent."[10]

Re-election

On February 6, 1855, the New York state legislature voted to reelect Seward to a second six-year term as senator. Cannons thundered outside the Albany capitol to announce the news. That night, great bonfires blazed in the streets in celebration. Antislavery leader

Theodore Parker wrote to Seward: "I hope the next six years may be as honorable to yourself and as profitable to the nation as are the last. . . . As you are the most powerful Senator in the United States, we shall look to you for heroic service."[11]

Returning to Washington for his second Senate term, Seward leased a handsome house on the corner of Twenty-first and G streets. Frances Seward, who disliked living in Washington, chose to remain in Auburn. In her absence, their son Frederick Seward's wife, Anna Wharton, agreed to serve as William Seward's official hostess. The Sewards loved giving fancy dinners for political friends, often followed by a game of cards. Guests sipped wine and enjoyed good conversation. An evening at the Sewards' was seldom boring.

Seward refused to make personal enemies. He tried to remain friendly, even with Southern senators. "Differences of opinion," he remarked, "even on the subject of slavery, with us are political, not social or personal, differences."[12] One day, Mississippi Senator Henry S. Foote threatened Seward with violence on the Senate floor. In response, Seward offered him a cheerful dinner invitation. On another day, Louisiana Senator Judah P. Benjamin condemned Seward in a speech. Seward promptly took him aside. "Benjamin," he calmly remarked, "give me a cigar, and when your speech is printed send me a copy."[13]

Each day, Seward rose early and enjoyed a walk before writing a letter home to Frances in Auburn. In 1850, he wrote, "I [have] had my walk, a visit to

the public greenhouse, my coffee and eggs, and the [newspaper,] and now indulge myself with a word to you, before beginning the studies of the day."[14]

The "Irrepressible Conflict"

The Kansas-Nebraska Act of 1854 allowed Kansas settlers to vote to decide whether their territory would allow slavery or not. Many Northerners, determined to make Kansas a free state, hurried west. Some Southerners also poured into the region, bringing their slaves with them. By the spring of 1856, violence had erupted in Kansas. The territory soon became known as Bleeding Kansas.

As national tensions increased over the issue of slavery, Seward joined a new political party, the Republicans, which formed in response to the Kansas-Nebraska Act. The Republicans opposed any extension of slavery beyond where it already existed. On October 25, 1858, in Rochester, New York, Seward spoke to an audience about the developing slavery crisis. "Shall I tell you what this collision means?" he declared.

> It is an irrepressible conflict between opposing and enduring forces, and it means that the United States must and will, sooner or later, become either entirely a slave-holding nation or entirely a free-labor nation. . . . I know, and you know, that a revolution has begun.[15]

Four months earlier, in Illinois, Abraham Lincoln had publicly spoken similar words: "'A house divided against itself cannot stand.' I believe this government cannot endure permanently half slave and half free."[16]

Lincoln's speech, which later became famous, failed to attract much notice at the time. Seward's "Irrepressible Conflict" speech, however, caused immediate comment nationwide.

Off to Europe

Seward needed a vacation. In May 1859, he suddenly chose to travel to Europe. Always concerned about her health, Frances Seward decided to remain at home. A great crowd cheered Seward as he boarded the ship *Ariel.* Sailing from New York City, he wrote to Frances: "The sky is bright, and the waters are calm. The ship is strong and swift."[17]

By May 20, Seward had arrived in London, England. The English entertained their famous visitor at dinners, receptions, and balls. Seward met Queen Victoria and thought her "a sturdy, small, unaffected and kind person."[18] Next, he traveled through France and to Rome and Naples in Italy. In Rome, Pope Pius IX granted him an audience. Sailing across the Mediterranean Sea, he visited Egypt and also took a side trip by sailboat to the city of Jaffa (present-day Tel Aviv, Israel). "For lack of chairs, we sit down on the deck," he wrote home, "and screen ourselves from the sun as well as we can by the shade of the sails."[19]

While Seward traveled, John Brown and his followers carried out a raid on a federal arsenal at Harpers Ferry, Virginia, in October 1859. Brown and his followers had hoped to start an armed slave rebellion. Captured and tried for treason, Brown was sentenced to hang. Many Southerners blamed Northern

antislavery leaders like Seward for John Brown's raid. Senator James Chesnut of South Carolina insisted that Seward had encouraged "much of the violence we have seen in the country."[20] An advertisement in a Richmond, Virginia, newspaper offered $50,000 for Seward's head. Antislavery Northerners declared that John Brown was a hero. Seward, however, wrote to his wife that he thought Brown had committed a crime.

On December 28, 1859, Seward's ship docked in New York City. A parade through snowy streets greeted him when he reached Auburn. Although he had traveled far and wide, Seward told his friends, it was "not until now that I have found the place which, above all others, I admire and love the best."[21]

5

PRESIDENTIAL CANDIDATE

William Seward had every reason to think he would win the Republican nomination for president in 1860. He was the most famous and experienced Republican politician in the United States. One Southern newspaper admitted,

> Mr. Seward is a great political leader. Unlike others who are willing to follow in the wake of popular sentiment, Seward leads. He stands head and shoulders above them all. . . . He is at once the greatest and most dangerous man in the government. . . . He has stood forth in the Senate of the United States, the great champion of freedom, and the stern opposer of slavery.[1]

In April 1860, New York Republicans chose seventy delegates to send to the Republican national convention. All seventy pledged their support to Seward.

Delegate Thurlow Weed became Seward's campaign manager. As he headed to Chicago, Illinois, for the convention, Weed stated, "I consider now that Seward's nomination and election are sure."[2]

Getting Support

Weed and the New York delegation arrived in Chicago on May 12. They proudly called themselves the "Irrepressibles," in reference to Seward's "Irrepressible Conflict" speech. Evidence of Weed's campaign work could be seen everywhere. Seward bands blared music in the Chicago streets, and Seward marchers paraded with colorful banners and badges.

Weed invited delegates from other states to visit his headquarters at the Richmond House Hotel. Weed smiled at everyone he met and shook hands heartily. "We think we have in Mr. Seward," he told one group, "just the qualities the country will need. He is known by us all as a statesman. . . . We expect to nominate him on the first ballot."[3] Delegates from Michigan, Wisconsin, Minnesota, California, and Massachusetts all pledged themselves to Seward.

Among the other candidates running for the nomination was Abraham Lincoln. Lincoln was very popular in Illinois, but he had little national reputation. Lincoln's campaign managers worked hard on his behalf. At the Lincoln headquarters at the Tremont House, newspaper reporter Murat Halstead described how "There are now at least a thousand men packed together in the halls of the Tremont House, crushing

Illinois lawyer Abraham Lincoln was a candidate for the Republican presidential nomination in 1860. Although Lincoln had served as a United States congressman in the 1840s, he was not as famous nationwide as Seward was.

each other's ribs, trampling each other's toes, and [spreading] the gossip of the day."[4] Lincoln's campaign managers may have promised delegates Cabinet posts and other government offices if Lincoln were nominated and elected. They insisted that Seward's political views were too radical. They claimed Seward would lose the national election if nominated.

Newspaper editor Horace Greeley did his best to keep Seward from winning support. In 1854, Greeley thought he should have been elected New York governor. He mistakenly blamed Seward for keeping him out of office. In Chicago, Republican convention delegates listened carefully when the famous newspaper editor declared that Seward was not a strong candidate for the nomination. Greeley claimed Seward was not widely supported in such key states as Pennsylvania, New Jersey, and Illinois.

Choosing a Candidate

Delegates met officially at the Wigwam, a great wooden building constructed especially for the convention. On May 17, thousands of cheering spectators thronged into the hall. "A very large share of the outside pressure [is] for Seward," observed Murat Halstead. "There is something almost irresistible here in the prestige of his fame."[5]

It was not considered appropriate in the 1800s for a candidate to campaign in person. Throughout the convention, Seward remained at home. Back in Auburn, he waited anxiously for the balloting results.

On May 18, he received a telegram from a few of the New York delegates: "All right. Everything indicates your nomination today sure."[6] That morning, the convention assembled to choose its candidate. Lincoln's campaign managers had secretly printed special entrance tickets. Crowds of Lincoln supporters were able to pack the Wigwam gallery. As a result, while Seward's name was warmly received, the response for Lincoln was overwhelming. One surprised reporter wrote, "Imagine all the hogs ever slaughtered in Cincinnati giving their death squeals together. . . . I thought the Seward yell could not be surpassed; but the Lincoln boys . . . made every plank and pillar in the building quiver."[7]

To win the nomination, a candidate needed 233 votes. On the first ballot, Seward received 173.5 votes, Lincoln 102, and the rest of the votes were scattered among other candidates. On the second ballot, Seward received 184.5 votes to 181 for Lincoln. Tensions mounted as a third round of balloting began. Four Massachusetts delegates surprisingly switched from Seward to Lincoln. Lincoln also picked up three votes from New Jersey and four more from Pennsylvania. Then the Ohio delegation gave Lincoln another fourteen votes. When the roll call ended, Seward's total had dropped to 180 and Lincoln's had jumped to 231.5, just a vote and a half short of the necessary total.

"A profound stillness," wrote one spectator, "fell upon the wigwam; the men ceased to talk and the ladies to flutter their fans; one could distinctly hear the scratching of pencils and the ticking of telegraph instruments on the reporters' tables."[8]

Soon, Ohio delegate D. K. Carrter rose and asked to be heard. The Ohioan announced a switch of four more votes in his delegation to Lincoln. The Republican convention had made its decision. Abraham Lincoln would be the presidential nominee. Lincoln's supporters wildly cheered and paraded in the aisles. Completely stunned, Thurlow Weed covered his face with his hands and wept.

Lincoln Nominated

It was a lovely spring day in Auburn. Seward was seated in his garden with a neighbor when he saw Dr. Theodore Dimon, an old friend, coming up the street with a telegram in his hand. Dimon solemnly handed the message to Seward. It read: "Lincoln nominated third ballot." Calmly, Seward read those four words and finally remarked, "Well, Mr. Lincoln will be elected and has some of the qualities to make a good President."[9]

At the Republican convention, Thurlow Weed, the master politician, had been outwitted by Lincoln's campaign managers. But Seward refused to criticize his friend. He soon told Weed, "You have my unbounded gratitude. . . . I wish that I were as sure that your sense of disappointment is as light as my own."[10] In truth, though, Seward felt shattered and believed his public career had come to an end. "I am without schemes, or plans, hopes, desires, or fears for the future," he sadly admitted.[11]

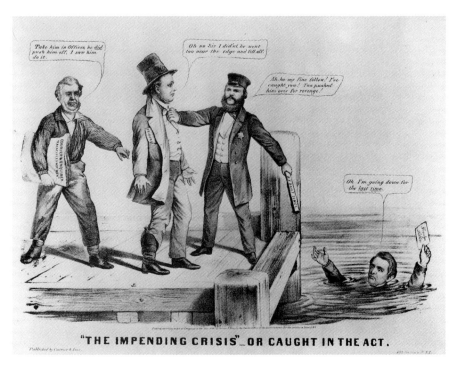

This political cartoon published by Currier and Ives appeared after Seward's defeat at the Republican National Convention in Chicago in 1860. Newspaper editor Horace Greeley (in top hat) is being accused of pushing Seward into the water. The drowning Seward is declaring, "Oh, I'm going down for the last time."

The Election of 1860

In time, Seward announced his full support for Lincoln's campaign. "Let the watchword of the Republican party be 'Union and Liberty,' and onward to victory," he declared.[12] In August 1860, he traveled through New England, Michigan, Wisconsin, Minnesota, Iowa, Kansas, and Illinois, giving campaign speeches supporting Lincoln.

Northern Democrats nominated Illinois Senator Stephen A. Douglas for president. Southern Democrats, however, feared Douglas would be too greatly influenced by Northern antislavery voters. Therefore, Southern Democrats, swayed by wealthy slaveholders, chose Vice President John C. Breckinridge as their presidential candidate. At the same time, the new Constitutional Union party nominated John Bell of Tennessee. The Constitutional Unionists took no stand on the slavery issue. They wanted only to hold the nation, which was rapidly dividing over the issues of slavery and states' rights, together at any cost.

With the Democrats so badly split, it seemed certain that Lincoln would be elected. Many Southerners hated the idea of an antislavery Republican president. One Georgia newspaper warned, "Let the consequences be what they may . . . the South will never submit to . . . the inauguration of Abraham Lincoln."[13]

In November, Lincoln did indeed win election with a majority of the electoral vote. Lincoln had repeatedly promised that he would not interfere with slavery where it existed. Nevertheless, within days of his election, many Southern slaveholders demanded that their states quit the Union.

Lincoln Makes an Offer

Seward returned to Washington on November 30, 1860, for the winter Senate session. Many of his friends felt certain that Lincoln would offer him a Cabinet position. "I shall await the development of

events and act as wisely as I can," he responded to these rumors.[14]

Secretary of state was the most important Cabinet office Lincoln needed to fill. Among his many duties, the secretary of state would handle all of the United States' relations with foreign countries. In December, Lincoln sent Seward two letters. The first formally announced his intention to name Seward as his secretary of state. In the second, Lincoln assured Seward that he truly wanted him for the job. "I now offer you the place," Lincoln stated, "in the hope that you will accept it, and with the belief that your position in the public eye, your integrity, ability, learning, and great experience, all combine to render it an appointment . . . fit to be made."[15]

On December 28, Seward wrote to Lincoln, accepting the post. "I will try to save freedom and my country," he told his wife.[16] Just eight days earlier, South Carolina had left the Union, protesting Lincoln's election as president. Other Southern states threatened to follow. Seward had little faith in Lincoln's political skills. He believed the future of the nation rested on his own shoulders. He told his wife, "I am the only hopeful, calm . . . person here."[17] Through January and February 1861, Seward tried to reason with excited congressmen in Washington. "Mad men North, and mad men South," he despaired, "are working together to produce [the ruin] of the Union by civil war."[18]

6

A NATION
TORN IN TWO

"The Nation looks to *you* . . . for its salvation," a concerned citizen wrote to Seward in 1861. "It is feared that Mr. [Lincoln] is not equal to the emergency of the times."[1] By February 1861, Mississippi, Alabama, Florida, Georgia, Louisiana, and Texas had joined South Carolina in seceding from the United States and setting up their own nation—the Confederate States of America.

Lincoln finally arrived in Washington, D.C., on the morning of February 23, 1861. He joined Seward that day for dinner. "He is very cordial and kind toward me—simple, natural, and agreeable," Seward remarked.[2] Lincoln gave Seward a draft of his inaugural address, asking for suggestions. Seward carefully read it and made several valuable comments. As the

days passed, however, Seward grew upset with some of Lincoln's choices for Cabinet positions. Seward thought he was wiser than Lincoln. He felt certain that he knew the best candidate for every job. He considered resigning, but finally thought better of the idea. He told his wife that he "did not dare to go home . . . and leave the country to chance."[3] On Inauguration Day, March 4, 1861, Abraham Lincoln took the oath of office as the sixteenth United States president. The following day, Seward was sworn in as secretary of state.

Lincoln's Diplomat

The State Department building stood on the corner of Fifteenth Street and Pennsylvania Avenue. It was the center of all the nation's diplomatic business with

Lincoln Sneaks Into Washington

Detective Allan Pinkerton believed Southern sympathizers planned to murder Lincoln when he changed trains in Baltimore, Maryland, on his journey to Washington, D.C. On February 22, Lincoln was persuaded to change his scheduled travel plans. He secretly took a train to the capital, while his official train traveled without him. Early the next morning, he arrived in Washington unannounced. There was no one at the station to greet him. The man about to be sworn in as president had slipped secretly into the city.

foreign countries. The State Department employed about one hundred people. Its staff included the keeper of the United States Seal, a historian, and a commissioner of patents.

Seward took two rooms on the second floor for his private offices. At his immediate command were chief clerk William Hunter and twenty-three clerks. Seward named his thirty-year-old son, Frederick, to be assistant secretary of state.

The State Department building stood at the corner of Fifteenth Street and Pennsylvania Avenue in Washington, D.C. It was here that Secretary of State Seward guided United States foreign policy during the Civil War.

Lincoln and Seward worked closely in choosing ministers to foreign countries. Minister was the title given to ambassadors in those days. Seward believed that Charles Francis Adams would be the best person to represent the United States as minister to Great Britain. Adams was the grandson of former President John Adams and the son of former President John Quincy Adams. Both John Adams and John Quincy Adams had also served as ministers to Great Britain. At Seward's urging, Lincoln sent Charles Francis Adams to Great Britain.

While fifty-nine-year-old Seward organized the State Department, newspaper reporter William Russell of the London *Times* visited him. Russell described Seward as "a slight, middle-sized man, of feeble build . . . [his] eyes secret but penetrating, and lively with humour . . . a subtle, quick man, rejoicing

in power . . . bursting with the importance of state mysteries."[4] Having been to Europe twice, Seward could understand

Frederick Seward, pictured here, proved very able in his position as assistant secretary of state. He often served as his father's private secretary and advised him on foreign affairs.

foreign cultures and the ways of the world. He also possessed a valuable diplomatic skill. He knew how to deal in a friendly way with people with whom he disagreed. Lincoln believed completely in his secretary of state. He made it clear that he planned to let Seward conduct the nation's foreign affairs.

Fort Pickens and Fort Sumter

During March and April 1861, the nation tottered on the brink of civil war. The seven Southern states that had left the United States had joined to form the Confederate States of America with Jefferson Davis as president. Throughout the South, Confederate soldiers were seizing federal forts and other federal property on Southern soil. Two important forts, however, Fort Pickens and Fort Sumter, remained in federal hands.

Seward urged that Fort Pickens, at the entrance to Pensacola Harbor on Florida's Gulf Coast, be reinforced and held. But he believed Fort Sumter, at the mouth of Charleston Harbor in South Carolina, was too weak to be defended. "I do not think it wise," Seward declared, "to provoke a civil war beginning at Charleston."[5] Seward suggested that federal troops abandon Fort Sumter.

"Some Thoughts for the President's Consideration"

For a few weeks, Lincoln remained undecided about Fort Sumter. In frustration, Seward decided that Lincoln had "no system, no relative ideas, no conception

of his situation."[6] Lincoln seemed confused. As a result, on April 1, 1861, Seward penned a letter to Lincoln. He titled it, "Some Thoughts for the President's Consideration." It suggested that the government was "without a policy, either domestic or foreign."

"Whatever policy we adopt," Seward's letter stated, "there must be an energetic prosecution of it. For this purpose, it must be somebody's business to pursue and direct it. . . . Either the President must do it himself . . . or [he should give the power to] some member of his Cabinet."[7] Seward ended his comments by gently offering to take on the responsibility himself.

Lincoln replied swiftly with a letter of his own. There *was* a national policy, he told Seward. He quoted his inaugural address, in which he promised "to hold, occupy and possess the property and places belonging to the government." As to foreign affairs, he pointed out that he and Seward had been preparing instructions to ministers "without even a suggestion that we had no foreign policy." In the end, Lincoln simply declared, "[Whatever] must be done, I must do it."[8] Seward realized that Lincoln intended to make all important decisions himself, including the refusal to evacuate Fort Sumter.

Civil War

On April 12, 1861, Confederate cannons began bombarding Fort Sumter. Two days later, the fort surrendered. Immediately, Lincoln called for volunteers

to put down the Southern rebellion. Within days, the slave states of Virginia, Arkansas, North Carolina, and Tennessee seceded from the Union and joined the Confederacy. North and south, patriotic people prepared for war. Teenage Fanny Seward wrote to her father from Auburn: "All is excitement here. . . . Flags are flying."[9]

In Washington, Seward rented a large brick house on Lafayette Park, close to the White House and the State Department. Once the home of a gentlemen's club called the Washington Club, it was still called the "Old Clubhouse." Seward moved in with his sons, Gus and Fred, and Fred's wife, Anna. Gus worked in Washington as a military paymaster.

At the State Department, Seward sent instructions to United States diplomats overseas. Southerners believed they could win independence, but realized they needed European help. Seward took on the responsibility of assuring that no foreign power would be allowed to interfere in American affairs.

Keeping Europe Neutral

Great Britain and France needed Southern cotton for their textile mills. Seward feared they would recognize Confederate independence simply to gain Southern cotton. Quickly, he instructed American ministers abroad to insist that the Civil War was a rebellion within the United States. The Confederacy, therefore, had no international rights. "They have misunderstood things fearfully, in Europe," he wrote to his wife. "Great Britain is in great danger of sympathizing so much with

the South, for the sake of peace and cotton, as to drive us to make war against her; as the ally of the traitors."[10]

Finally, on May 13, 1861, the British government issued a proclamation of neutrality. Great Britain planned to remain strictly neutral in the warfare "unhappily commenced between the government of the United States and certain states styling themselves the Confederate States of America."[11] The British realized it would be unwise to risk war with the United States. Within a few weeks, France, Spain, the Netherlands, Prussia, and other nations followed Great Britain's example. On June 1, 1861, Great Britain also announced that Confederate warships would not be allowed to enter British ports. British Foreign Minister Lord John Russell quietly commented, "If it can possibly be helped, Mr. Seward must not be allowed to get [Great Britain] into a quarrel."[12]

Union and Confederate troops clashed near a creek called Bull Run near Manassas, Virginia, on July 21, 1861. The North suffered a stunning defeat in its first big battle. Immediately, Seward sent hopeful letters abroad to American diplomats. "You will receive the account of [our defeat] at Manassas," he wrote. "The shock, however, has passed away. . . . The heart of the country is sound."[13] To Frances he confided, "Nothing remains but to reorganize and begin again."[14]

Seward's Bell

The United States Constitution allows for the arrest of citizens suspected of disloyalty during a rebellion.

In July 1861, President Lincoln put Seward in charge of making necessary arrests. Seward enjoyed having the power. One day, he boasted to a visitor, "I can touch a bell on my right hand and order the imprisonment of a citizen of Ohio; I can touch the bell again and order the imprisonment of a citizen of New York; and no power on earth, except that of the President, can release them."[15]

Seward promptly arrested men and women suspected of giving aid or comfort to the enemy or even openly expressing sympathy with the South. Prisoners included newspaper editors and political leaders. A person suspected of disloyalty was often seized at night and imprisoned in the nearest fort. In August 1861, Seward sent one typical telegram:

> *[To] John A. Kennedy, Superintendent of Police, New York:*
>
> *Arrest Charles Kopperl, of Carroll County, Mississippi, now in your city, and send him to Fort Lafayette.*
>
> *William H. Seward.*[16]

By October 14, 1861, Seward had arrested as many as two hundred people. Most lay in dank cells at Fort Lafayette in New York Harbor or at Fort Warren in Boston. Only if a prisoner swore allegiance to the United States and promised not to aid or encourage the Confederates could he or she be freed. Seward held this power until February 14, 1862, when Lincoln turned over responsibility for political prisoners to the War Department.

The *Trent* Affair

On the afternoon of November 8, 1861, in the waters off the Bahama Islands, near Florida, the United States warship *San Jacinto* fired a warning shot. The cannonball splashed across the path of the British mail ship *Trent*. The British vessel halted, and United States Navy Captain Charles Wilkes sent an armed boarding party onto its deck. Among the passengers, they found James Mason, John Slidell, and their two secretaries. All four were taken prisoner. Mason and Slidell were Confederate diplomats on their way to Great Britain and France.

Throughout the North, news of the arrests brought cheering crowds into the streets. "We do not believe the American heart ever thrilled with more genuine delight," exclaimed *The New York Times*.[17] Seward was at first pleased over the capture of men he regarded as traitors. But William Dayton, United States minister to France, soon wrote him a letter:

> It is very evident . . . that upon *this question* we will have scarcely a friend among the press or public men in Europe. The impression here, as in England, is . . . that *we are a power reckless of the obligations of international law. . . .* I have been asked by intelligent gentlemen here why it was that *you* seemed so determined "to pick a quarrel" with England.[18]

The British regarded the arrests as a terrible insult to the British flag. The British government demanded the immediate release of Mason and Slidell. The United States and Great Britain suddenly seemed to be on the

verge of war. Within three weeks, ten thousand British troops boarded ships bound for Canada. The Confederates felt confident the *Trent* affair would win them Great Britain as an ally. If this happened, Confederate victory and independence seemed certain.

Seward quickly realized the danger. He decided that Mason and Slidell should be released. But Lincoln was reluctant to do so. The president and his secretary of state failed to agree when they reviewed the case. Lincoln told him, "You will go on, of course, preparing your answer, which, as I understand it, will state the reasons why they ought to be given up. Now, I have a mind to try my hand at stating the reasons why they ought *not* to be given up. We will compare the points on each side."[19]

Seward carefully prepared his arguments. At a Cabinet meeting, he told Lincoln that to go to war with Great Britain would be "to abandon all hope of [putting down] the rebellion."[20] Such a war would greatly endanger American ships at sea and bankrupt the national treasury. Finally, on December 26, 1861, Lincoln yielded to Seward's arguments. Within days, Mason and Slidell stepped from their cells at Fort Warren in Boston. They boarded a British ship and continued on their journey to Europe.

Seward had shown courage in taking the unpopular view of releasing Mason and Slidell. On both sides of the Atlantic, people felt relieved that the *Trent* affair had ended. The *New York Tribune* declared, "We believe the [government] is stronger with the people to-day than if Mason and Slidell had never been

captured or their surrender had been refused."[21] Seward proudly wrote to Weed of his success. "You will see what has been done," he crowed. "You will know who did it."[22]

Seward and Lincoln

Lincoln rarely made an important decision without consulting his secretary of state. When Seward missed Cabinet meetings, Secretary of the Navy Gideon Welles admitted that there was "a reluctance to discuss . . . any great decision without him."[23] By spring 1862, a strong personal friendship had grown between Seward and Lincoln. Seward had come to like and respect Lincoln. "The President," he wrote to his wife, "is the best of us all."[24]

Seward often visited the White House. He was especially fond of the Lincoln boys, Tad and Willie, and he gave them two pet cats. President Lincoln often visited Seward at home as well. In the Seward parlor, the two men would sit in front of the fire and talk. Both men were lawyers, both were skilled story-tellers, and each had a fine sense of humor. Seward always enjoyed hearing one of Lincoln's stories, and Seward's constant cheerfulness often raised Lincoln's spirits.

Seward and the Troops

"I am counseling with the Cabinet one hour, with the Army officers the next, the Navy next, and I visit all the troops as fast as they come," Seward once declared.[25] Seward often took carriage rides out to the

Union forts and camps surrounding Washington, D.C. He also actively took part in raising army volunteers. To increase enlistments, Seward persuaded Secretary of War Edwin Stanton to give new recruits a twenty-five-dollar bounty when they entered service. When New Yorkers organized a new regiment, the 103rd, in 1862, they called it the "Seward Infantry" in honor of the secretary of state.

Emancipation

At first, most Northern soldiers fought the Civil War only to reunite the nation. But Seward never forgot his desire to bring an end to slavery. He supported Lincoln's executive order that ended slavery in Washington, D.C. He also called for the use of African Americans in the Union Army. In April 1862, Seward

The Homestead Act
In the midst of the Civil War, Congress passed the Homestead Act of 1862. The new law offered one hundred sixty acres of free public land to anyone who would live on it and develop it for five years. Thousands of foreigners flocked to the United States to take advantage of the offer. Along with American settlers, they established farms and towns throughout the American West. Seward called the Homestead Act "one of the most important steps ever taken by any government toward [promoting] the universal brotherhood of nations."[26]

arranged a treaty with Great Britain. The United States and Great Britain agreed to try to stop slave trading by other foreign nations.

At a Cabinet meeting on July 22, 1862, President Lincoln raised the subject of an emancipation proclamation. He wished to free all slaves belonging to the Southern enemy. Seward approved the idea, but he questioned the timing of such a proclamation after a summer of Union battlefield defeats. "It may be viewed," he argued, "as the last measure of an exhausted government, a cry for help . . . our last *shriek*, on the retreat."[27] Seward thought Lincoln

Abraham Lincoln reads the Emancipation Proclamation to his Cabinet in 1862. F. B. Carpenter's famous painting of the scene hangs today in the United States Capitol.

should wait until the Union Army won a victory. Lincoln realized his secretary of state was right. He put his proclamation aside and waited.

Union success in forcing the Southerners to end their attempted invasion of the North at the bloody Battle of Antietam in Maryland in September 1862 finally provided Lincoln with his opportunity. On September 24, he issued the preliminary Emancipation Proclamation, announcing that all the slaves of those places in rebellion against the United States as of January 1, 1863, would be "thenceforward and forever free."[28] Lincoln hoped the fear of losing their slaves would persuade some Southern states to quit fighting and rejoin the Union.

News of the Emancipation Proclamation flashed across Europe and caused excitement. An American in Paris wrote to Seward, "France is unanimously for emancipation, and our cause will now daily grow in grace here."[29] In Great Britain, too, common people recognized the justice of freeing the slaves. By making slavery a war issue, Lincoln won the moral support of many Europeans.

A Cabinet Crisis

A December 6, 1862, newspaper article in the *Boston Commonwealth* demanded, "Remove him! William H. Seward stands before the American people today as the enemy of the public. . . . Let the Watchword for the Hour be, *Remove Seward from the Cabinet!*"[30] Other newspapers agreed. Seward found himself being blamed for every weakness in the government

and every Union defeat on the battlefield. Seward had urged Lincoln to replace the ineffective Union General George McClellan. McClellan's many supporters were resentful. In the minds of many, Seward simply had too much influence over Lincoln. At the same time, Treasury Secretary Salmon P. Chase secretly yearned to be elected president in 1864. Chase's Republican friends in the Senate wished to weaken Lincoln politically by getting rid of Seward.

On December 17, 1862, four days after the Union defeat at the Battle of Fredericksburg, Republican senators passed a resolution calling for Lincoln to reorganize his Cabinet. "They may do as they please about me," Seward angrily responded, "but they shall not put the President in a false position on my account."[31] He swiftly penned a letter of resignation. When Lincoln visited him soon afterward, Seward insisted that it would be a relief to leave office. "Ah, yes," Lincoln told him, ". . . that will do very well for you, but I . . . can't get out."[32]

Lincoln soon realized that Republican senators wanted Seward out of the Cabinet so that Treasury Secretary Chase could rise in power in his place. On December 19, while Seward packed, Lincoln met with nine senators as well as members of his Cabinet at the White House. Throughout the long meeting, Lincoln defended his right to choose his own Cabinet.

Afterward, Chase, in embarrassment, offered his own resignation. Lincoln's eyes lit up. "Let me have it," he said. He snatched the written resignation from

Chase's hands. "I can dispose of this subject now," he happily declared. "I see my way clear."[33] With resignation letters from both Seward and Chase he could keep both men or let them both go, as he chose. Cheerfully, he told New York Senator Ira Harris, "I can ride now—I've got a pumpkin in each end of my [saddle]bag."[34] He had foiled the political plot against his trusted secretary of state. Lincoln would eventually accept Chase's resignation in 1864. But he wanted to keep Seward in his Cabinet to the end.

7

LINCOLN'S RIGHT HAND

M r. Seward," stated *The New York Times*, ". . . has attended exclusively to the affairs of his own department, and has sustained, with cheerful and hearty loyalty, whatever measures the President has deemed essential to the public good."[1]

During 1863, Seward guided the course of America's foreign relations. He wrote hundreds of letters to United States diplomats around the world. He also kept in contact with foreign diplomats stationed in Washington, D.C. To the British Embassy alone he sent at least one thousand letters.

The Laird Rams

The Confederates believed that, if they could purchase warships abroad, they could ruin United States

commerce. Private manufacturers in Great Britain secretly found ways to get around their country's policy of neutrality. The Confederate ship *Florida*, which was built in Great Britain, steamed into action in January 1863. During the next fifteen months, the *Florida* destroyed thirty-two Northern vessels.

It was the Confederate warship *Alabama*, however, that brought Great Britain and the United States close to war once again. Built in Liverpool, England, the *Alabama* sailed the Atlantic and Pacific oceans in search of United States merchant ships. In a year and a half, the *Alabama* captured or destroyed as many as sixty American vessels. Not until June 19, 1864, was the *Alabama* sunk after a fiery battle with the U.S.S. *Kearsarge* off the coast of France.

The same Liverpool shipyard that built the *Alabama* began constructing two ironclad ships, called "Laird rams." These ships also appeared to be intended for the Confederacy. They were scheduled to be launched in August 1863. Seward wrote to Minister Charles Francis Adams: "Can the British government suppose for a moment that such an assault as is thus [planned] can be made upon us by British-built, armed, and manned vessels without at once arousing the whole nation and making . . . war inevitable?"[2] In meetings with British Foreign Minister Lord John Russell, Adams calmly pointed out the danger of war over this issue.

Russell responded on September 8, 1863, with a formal note: "Lord Russell presents his compliments to Mr. Adams, and has the honor to inform him that

instructions have been issued which will prevent the departure of the two iron-clad vessels from Liverpool."[3] The Laird rams would not be allowed to leave England. They were seized by British authorities on October 9. Another international disaster had been avoided.

Seward the Tour Guide

In Seward's view, foreign powers had no idea how great the resources of the North were. To educate them, he invited Washington's foreign diplomats on a grand tour of New York State. Ambassadors from Great Britain, France, Russia, and several other countries accepted. The War Department provided a special railroad car, and Seward acted as tour guide. He took the group up the Hudson River to Albany and Schenectady in July 1863. Visits to Syracuse, Utica, and Auburn followed. The gentlemen took boat rides on the Finger Lakes and visited Niagara Falls. Throughout New York State, Seward showed them how strong the American economy remained in the midst of civil war. Machinery thumped and whined at busy factories and mills. Crops ripened in farmers' fields. Seward charmed his guests, and they returned to Washington convinced that the North could win the war. Richard Pemell, Lord Lyons, the British minister, fully enjoyed the tour. He said of Seward, "When one comes really to know him one is surprised to find much to esteem and even to like in him."[4]

The Turning Point

In one great battle, Confederate General Robert E. Lee still hoped to defeat the North and gain recognition and help from Great Britain and France. In June 1863, Lee marched his army into Pennsylvania. They clashed with the Union troops of General George Meade at the Battle of Gettysburg. From July 1 to July 3, roaring cannons sent shells whistling through

Dead soldiers lie on the field after the Battle of Gettysburg, which took place from July 1–3, 1863, in Pennsylvania. While Americans fought to decide the future of the nation, Secretary of State Seward used his diplomatic skills to keep Great Britain and France out of the war.

the air. Soldiers fired muskets and thousands of men fell dead and wounded. In the end, the Union troops held their ground.

As the beaten Confederates retreated back to Virginia, it was clear that the tide of the war had turned. In November, Seward joined Lincoln on a visit to Gettysburg, Pennsylvania. There, Lincoln gave his famed Gettysburg Address, dedicating a cemetery to the battlefield dead.

Events of 1864

President Lincoln had given General Ulysses S. Grant command of all Union armies by 1864. In Virginia, Grant fought a series of battles that forced Robert E. Lee's Confederate army back toward the Confederate capital of Richmond.

Thanksgiving Day
In the fall of 1863, Seward approached the president with a suggestion. For many years, the country had observed a Thanksgiving Day in the autumn. However, each state had always chosen its own day to celebrate. Seward suggested that Lincoln proclaim a day of national thanksgiving. Lincoln agreed, making only a few changes in the proclamation Seward offered. As a result, the last Thursday in November has become the national Thanksgiving Day.

Elsewhere, at the Battle of Monocacy in Maryland on July 9, 1864, Seward's son, Lieutenant Colonel Will Seward, fell wounded. As soon as he got the news, Seward hurried by carriage into Maryland to search for him. He could not find his son, but he soon met soldiers from Will's regiment. They described Will's bravery in battle and assured the secretary of state that his son was not seriously wounded.

In June 1864, Republicans nominated Lincoln for a second term as president. Democrats picked General George McClellan to run against Lincoln. On November 8, 1864, Seward joined Lincoln in the War Department telegraph office. Together they waited for voting results to arrive. In the end, the Northern people chose to trust in Lincoln's continued leadership. When Lincoln's re-election became certain, Seward addressed a crowd gathered in front of his house. "Henceforth all men will come to see [Lincoln] as you and I have seen him," he declared, "—a true, loyal, patient, patriotic, and [generous] man. . . . Abraham Lincoln will take his place with Washington and Franklin and Jefferson and Adams and Jackson. . . ."[5]

The Hampton Roads Conference

By January 1865, the Union army of General William T. Sherman had marched across Georgia and was pushing into South Carolina. In Virginia, General Robert E. Lee's Confederate army at Richmond grew weaker day by day. In a last attempt to save the Confederacy, Confederate President Jefferson Davis sent Vice

President Alexander Stephens, Senator and ex-Secretary of State R.M.T. Hunter, and Assistant Secretary of War John A. Campbell north to discuss chances for peace. Lincoln and Seward met these Confederate commissioners at Hampton Roads, Virginia. Hampton Roads was the name given to the mouth of the James River, where so much shipping traveled back and forth. On February 3, 1865, the five men sat together for four hours, aboard the Union steamboat *River Queen*.

The meeting was friendly. Lincoln promised to act kindly toward the South when the war was over. But he made it clear that there could be no peace until Southerners surrendered their armies, freed their slaves, and rejoined the United States. Seward fully agreed. Earlier he had stated, "The government can afford to be liberal on other points, but it cannot yield anything on the point that the Union must be maintained, or on the point [that] African slavery must now cease to exist."[6] The Confederates left the meeting disappointed that they had gained nothing.

A Carriage Accident

The Confederate government collapsed on April 2, 1865, when Confederate troops finally abandoned Richmond and retreated westward. Cheering Union soldiers soon swarmed into the Confederate capital. After four hard years, it seemed the end of the war was near.

On the warm spring afternoon of April 5, Seward left the State Department for a relaxing carriage ride

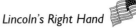

with his son Fred, his daughter Fanny, and Fanny's friend Mary Titus. As they rolled along the road, they noticed that the carriage door would not stay closed. The coachman stopped to repair the latch, when the unattended horses suddenly bolted and ran. As the carriage sped wildly, sixty-three-year-old Seward tried to reach out and gather the reins. He lost his balance and fell heavily onto the road. The horses galloped onward, carrying the coach toward Lafayette Park. A soldier stepped forward and finally halted the frightened animals.

When help arrived, Seward was discovered lying unconscious in the dusty road. He was carefully lifted and carried back to his house. Doctors realized Seward had suffered serious injuries. His jaw was fractured on both sides, his face bruised and swollen. His right shoulder was dislocated and his right arm was broken. Frances Seward in Auburn received the news by telegraph and hurried immediately to Washington. "I find Henry worse than I had anticipated," she wrote her sister. "It makes my heart ache to look at him."[7]

While Seward lay injured at home, Secretary of War Edwin Stanton often visited. Though normally a gruff man, Stanton gave Seward gentle attention. As a nurse, Fanny Seward noted, Stanton was "much more efficient than [I was] who did not know what to do."[8]

One day, Abraham Lincoln also visited. The president had been with the Union Army in Virginia when he learned of Seward's accident.

"You are back from Richmond?" whispered Seward, who could hardly speak.

"Yes," said Lincoln, "and I think we are near the end, at last."

Lincoln stretched his long body across the foot of Seward's bed and rested on his elbow. He quietly told the injured secretary of state about his tour of Richmond. "They were left together for half an hour or more," remembered Fred Seward. "Then the door opened softly, and Mr. Lincoln came out gently, [showing] by a silent look and gesture that Seward had fallen into a feverish slumber."[9]

Sadly, Seward and Lincoln would never meet again.

8

THE NIGHT OF HORROR

"A ssassination is not an American practice," Seward had once insisted.[1] After all, no American president had ever been assassinated. But Seward did not know the mind of John Wilkes Booth. Booth was an actor born in Maryland and fiercely loyal to the South. Since November 1864, Booth had been plotting to kidnap Lincoln. He believed the Confederate government could trade Lincoln for thousands of Confederate prisoners of war.

Then on April 9, 1865, Robert E. Lee surrendered his Confederate army at Appomattox Court House, Virginia. Suddenly, Booth decided on a different goal. He vowed to have Lincoln, Vice President Andrew Johnson, and Secretary of State Seward assassinated. Booth believed these killings would disrupt the United

States government, give hope to the Confederacy, and make him famous.

At the Washington boardinghouse of Mary Surratt, he made his hurried plans on April 14. Booth announced that he would assassinate Abraham Lincoln himself. He gave fellow plotter George Atzerodt the task of killing Vice President Johnson. The job of murdering Seward was assigned to Lewis Paine, an ex-Confederate soldier.

A Strange Messenger

At his home, Seward slowly recovered from his carriage accident in his third floor bedroom. On April 14, he was able to chew solid food for the first time. Fanny Seward read to him in the afternoon. In the evening, the sounds of happy shouting and singing came in through the bedroom window. A torchlight parade at the White House was celebrating the end of the war. A band played "Rally Round the Flag," and fireworks lit up Lafayette Park. Seward rested on his bed in a position that eased the pain of his broken arm. His daughter sat in the room with him. An army nurse, Sergeant George Robinson, was also there to watch over him at night.

At 10:00 P.M., the front doorbell rang. Servant William Bell opened the door and discovered a stranger wearing a light overcoat. The stranger explained he was a messenger and brought some medicine from Seward's doctor. He insisted he had to deliver the medicine to Seward in person. Bell responded that no

one was allowed upstairs, but the stranger pushed his way into the house and started up the staircase.

From his room upstairs, Fred Seward later recalled, "Hearing the noise of footsteps in the hall, I came out and met him." The strange messenger repeated that he had to see Seward personally. Fred told the man, "I am his son, and the Assistant Secretary of State. Go back and tell the doctor I refused to let you go into the sickroom, because Mr. Seward was sleeping." The man, who was Lewis Paine, replied, "Very well, sir, I will go."[2]

Turning away, Paine slowly started down the stairs. In another instant, however, he reached into his coat and pulled out a heavy pistol. He pointed it at Fred and pulled the trigger. The hammer clicked, but the gun failed to fire. With furious energy, Paine raised the weapon and smashed Fred twice over the head. The noise of the attack carried into Seward's bedroom. Either Fanny or Sergeant Robinson opened the door to see what was happening. Paine threw down the pistol and drew a large Bowie knife. He struck at Robinson, knocked him down, pushed Fanny aside, and rushed into the bedroom.

In the dim light, Paine spied Seward lying in his bed. He hurried to the bedside and slashed repeatedly at the helpless figure. Robinson later declared, "I saw him strike Mr. Seward [and cut him] twice that I am sure of; the first time he struck him on the right cheek, and then he seemed to be cutting around his neck."[3]

The frenzied assassin slashed and hacked. Seward rolled to the floor wrapped in his bedsheets, blood gushing from his wounds. At the same time, Robinson bravely jumped upon Paine and tried to pull him away. The sergeant suffered a wound in the shoulder.

Thirty-eight-year-old Gus Seward, awakened by the noise, joined Robinson in the struggle. Paine began shouting, "I'm mad [insane]! I'm mad!"[4] Fanny screamed for help, and William Bell, the servant, rushed out of the house, also yelling for help. Frances Seward, hearing the screaming, stepped from her room, staring about in frightened confusion. Finally, Paine wrestled himself free from Robinson, struck Gus in the forehead, and bolted down the stairs. State Department messenger Emerick Hansell had entered the house by this time and was climbing the stairs. Paine stabbed Hansell, inflicting a serious wound in his side, and escaped into the street.

The Bloody Aftermath

News of the attack on Seward quickly spread. Secretary of War Edwin Stanton was at home preparing for bed, when his wife called from downstairs, "Mr. Seward is murdered!"

"Humbug," Stanton replied. "I left him only an hour ago."[5] He pulled on his clothes again and hurried to the Seward home.

A messenger brought Secretary of the Navy Gideon Welles the same horrible news. "Damn the rebels, this is their work," Welles exclaimed.[6] He also rushed off to Seward's. Welles discovered soldiers and bystanders

crowded outside the Seward house. He pushed his way past and joined Stanton at the door.

The two Cabinet officers went inside and climbed the blood-splattered staircase. They learned that Seward and Fred were both seriously injured. Stanton immediately ordered soldiers to guard the house. Then he and Welles hurried on to Ford's Theatre on Tenth Street. More shocking news had arrived. President Lincoln had been shot by John Wilkes Booth while attending a play called *Our American Cousin*.

At their home, the Seward family remained stunned by Paine's violent attack. Blood was everywhere. "My dress was stained with it," Fanny said. "Mother's was dabbled with it—it was on everything."[7] When the family doctor arrived, he feared at first that the jugular vein in Seward's neck had been severed, because there was so much bleeding. Luckily, this was not the case. Two additional doctors soon reached the scene. The doctors sewed Seward's deepest cuts and bandaged him.

The most seriously injured was Fred Seward. Paine's blows had opened Fred's skull so badly his brain could be seen in two places. Fred would remain in a coma for several days. Weeks would pass before it seemed hopeful that he would live.

"I Am a *Bruised* Reed"

In a single night of horror, John Wilkes Booth had murdered Abraham Lincoln, and Lewis Paine had nearly killed William Seward. Only George Atzerodt had failed to carry out his mission to kill Vice President

The Death of Lincoln

John Wilkes Booth fired a bullet into Abraham Lincoln's brain at Ford's Theatre on the night of April 14, 1865. Then Booth leaped onto the stage and escaped out a back door. Soldiers carried the unconscious president from Ford's Theatre across the street to the boardinghouse of William Petersen. In a back bedroom, they put Lincoln on a bed. Through the night, grief-stricken family members and government officials kept a death watch. At 7:22 A.M. on April 15, 1865, Abraham Lincoln died.

Andrew Johnson. He lacked the nerve to attack Johnson and got drunk instead. On the morning of April 15, 1865, Johnson was sworn in as the seventeenth United States president.

Seward began a slow recovery. For weeks he suffered from double vision. With broken jaws from his carriage accident and slashed cheeks from Paine's knife attack, he could not speak without pain. Instead he chalked messages on a slate.

Lincoln's death plunged the nation into mourning. The Seward family tried to keep the tragic news from the injured secretary of state. Within days of Paine's attack, however, Seward asked to be propped up in bed. He wished to see the spring leaves from his bedroom window. Instead he saw flags outside flying at half-mast. He immediately understood that Lincoln was dead. "If he had been alive, he would have been

the first to call on me," he remarked, "but he has not been here . . . and there is the flag at half mast."[8]

By April 24, newspaper reporter Noah Brooks could write, "All the wounded in the Seward mansion are slowly recovering. . . . The [strength] of the elder Seward, who is now quite old, is amazing."[9] Sixty-three-year-old Seward still looked terrible. His right arm remained bound in a sling. His face was swollen and scarred by the wounds. An iron frame held his broken jaw in place and made speech difficult. Assistant Secretary of War Charles A. Dana described the secretary of state as "one of the most horrible spectacles that the human eye ever beheld."[10]

"I am a *bruised* reed," Seward admitted, "and the marvel is that I am not broken in pieces."[11] But President Johnson requested that he continue as secretary of state. *The New York Times* declared that Johnson regarded "the [saving] of the Secretary's life as second to that of no man in the nation, and impatiently awaits the time when he will have the benefit of Mr. Seward's counsel."[12]

Seward slowly resumed his duties at the State Department. At the end of May, he began attending Cabinet meetings. By July, he was able to spend five hours a day at his office, and in good weather he started taking carriage rides again.

Frances Seward nursed both her husband and her son Fred with loving care. Sadly, though, she finally fell victim to her own poor health. She died on June 21, 1865, nine weeks after Paine's assault, at the age of fifty-nine.

The Fate of the Conspirators

Detectives arrested Lewis Paine at Mary Surratt's boardinghouse on April 16, 1865. He was dressed as a laborer and claimed he was there to dig a sewer. Nervously, Mary Surratt denied that Paine was working for her. Caught in a lie, the detectives soon identified Paine as Seward's attacker and locked him in wrist-irons. George Atzerodt, David Herold, and Mary Surratt were also arrested as suspected members of Booth's murder conspiracy. On April 26, Union cavalrymen cornered John Wilkes Booth in a tobacco barn near Bowling Green, Virginia. When Booth refused to surrender, Sergeant Boston Corbett took aim and shot at him. The bullet struck Lincoln's assassin in the neck and killed him.

In May, Washington citizens crowded into a courtroom to watch the trial of the suspected conspirators. Reporter Noah Brooks observed Paine at the trial. "He

Lewis Paine is seen wearing the same clothes he wore the night he attacked Seward in his bed. A loyal Confederate, Paine had served as a soldier in a Florida regiment before joining John Wilkes Booth's murder conspiracy.

The convicted conspirators—Mary Surratt, Lewis Paine, David Herold, and George Atzerodt—hang from the gallows at Washington's Arsenal Penitentiary on July 7, 1865. So many spectators wished to witness the hanging that special tickets were printed for admittance into the prison yard.

sat bolt upright against the wall," noted Brooks, "looming up like a young giant above the others."[13] All through the trial, Paine refused to talk to detectives. One of the military judges was heard to remark, "Paine seems to want to be hung, so I guess we might as well hang him."[14] On June 30, Paine was sentenced to death, along with George Atzerodt, David Herold, and Mary Surratt. The four convicted conspirators were hanged at Washington's Arsenal Penitentiary on July 7, 1865.

9

RECONSTRUCTION

"W" ho is now to lead this country back to
peace . . . and union?" Seward wondered.[1] The
assassination of Abraham Lincoln swiftly changed atti-
tudes in the North. In his second inaugural address,
Lincoln had stated, "With malice toward none, with
charity for all . . . let us strive on to finish the work
we are in; to bind up the nation's wounds."[2] Now,
however, there were Northerners who demanded harsh
punishment for the South.

While these Northerners raged, Seward remained
kindhearted. "History shows," he had once remarked,
"that the more generous . . . the conqueror to the conquered, the sooner victory has been followed by . . . a
lasting peace."[3]

Binding Wounds

It was the responsibility of the State Department to process pardons for those Confederate officers and government officials who wanted them. Many Confederates applied directly to Seward for pardons either at the State Department or at his house. "They come to me," he wrote in August 1865, "as if I were more inclined to tenderness than others, because I have been calm and cool under political excitement."[4]

When Confederate leader R.M.T. Hunter visited Washington, Seward warmly greeted him and invited him to dinner. At the dinner table, the Virginian found under his plate an official pardon signed and sealed. By the end of 1865, Seward had obtained pardons for dozens of Confederate leaders. "Once we were friends," Seward reminded citizens. "We have since been enemies. We are friends again. But whether . . . in peace, or in war, we are, and can be nothing else . . . than [brothers]."[5]

The work of reuniting the states after the Civil War became known as Reconstruction. President Andrew Johnson and Secretary of State Seward viewed Reconstruction in much the same way. Johnson, like Lincoln, intended to be lenient with the South. "The South longs to come home," Seward reminded people. "Those who refuse to take them into the family again are in my opinion guilty of a great crime."[6]

Even before the end of the war, it was obvious that many Republicans in Congress held a different view.

Following the Civil War, President Andrew Johnson decided to be generous toward the conquered Southern states.

They became known as Radical Republicans. The Radical Republicans believed the South should be punished harshly for fighting a brutal war to protect slavery. They refused to allow white Southern politicians the right to reorganize their state governments or to reenter Congress. A few Radical Republicans in the Cabinet showed where they stood. Rather than obey Johnson's policies, Postmaster General William Dennison, Attorney General James Speed, and Secretary of the Interior James Harlan all resigned in July. Seward, however, remained loyal to the president.

The Swing Around the Circle

As the 1866 congressional elections approached, President Johnson decided to conduct a whirlwind speaking tour across the North. Union war heroes General Ulysses S. Grant and Admiral David Farragut agreed to travel with the president. Secretary of State Seward and Secretary of the Navy Gideon Welles also boarded the special train. Johnson's political tour became known as the Swing Around the Circle.

Leaving Washington on August 28, 1866, the group journeyed to Philadelphia, New York City, and Chicago, then on to St. Louis, Missouri, and Louisville, Kentucky. At first, large crowds applauded President Johnson's speeches. In strong language, Johnson condemned the Radical Republicans. In time, hecklers appeared in the crowds. Their insults only made Johnson more angry and stubborn in his attitude.

After leaving Louisville, Kentucky, on the return journey to Washington, Seward suddenly fell deathly

ill with the bacterial disease cholera. President Johnson later entered Seward's railroad car to find out how he was. Though terribly sick, Seward grasped Johnson's hand and whispered, "My mind is clear, and I wish to say at this time that your course is right." Seward had supported the president, "and if my life is spared," he promised, "I shall continue to do so."[7]

An army ambulance waited for Seward at the Washington railroad station. Back home, he began a slow recovery. Twenty-one-year-old Fanny Seward nursed her father as well as she could. But Fanny was suffering from tuberculosis. In October 1866, Seward wept upon learning that his beloved daughter had died.

The Radical Republicans

The Swing Around the Circle failed to win President Johnson much support. In the November 1866 elections, the Radical Republicans gained control of Congress. Increasingly, the Republicans blamed Seward for everything wrong with Andrew Johnson's administration. "I mourn over Andy," wrote Maine Senator William Fessenden. "He began by meaning well, but I fear that Seward's evil counsels have carried him beyond the reach of salvation."[8] Johnson had once sided with the Radicals, said Radical Congressman Thaddeus Stevens, "but Seward entered into him, and ever since they have both been running down steep places into the sea."[9] *Nation* magazine wrote of Seward, "Distrusted by his old friends. . . . He wanders around like a ghost—a leader without a party."[10]

President Andrew Johnson is mocked in this 1866 political cartoon. Johnson is shown as a stern Roman emperor unmoved by the turmoil going on below him. Behind his throne stands chief advisor William Seward. Many Republicans believed Seward was a bad influence on the president.

Seward did seem like a different man. The deaths of Abraham Lincoln, his wife Frances, his daughter Fanny, and his own severe wounding had all deeply shocked him. All this sadness and the stress of Reconstruction nearly broke Seward's spirit.

In the autumn of 1866, the State Department moved from its location near the White House to a building at Fourteenth Street and S Street, a mile from Seward's house. Instead of walking to his office each morning, Secretary Seward now had to take a

carriage ride. One young man who visited Seward noticed how depressed and tired he had become: "Although his manner was as . . . kind as ever, and his talk as free, he appeared to have closed his account with the public; he no longer seemed to care."[11]

Archduke Maximilian

International affairs still required Seward's attention. French Emperor Napoleon III had dreamed for a long time of establishing a world empire. In June 1863, he sent French troops to occupy Mexico. Napoleon III installed Archduke Maximilian of Austria on the Mexican throne. The French emperor knew he could influence the policies of Archduke Maximilian. It was against United States policy to allow European governments to interfere with countries in the Western Hemisphere. But during the Civil War, the United States was too distracted to complain. "Nations no more than individuals can wisely divide their attention upon many subjects at one time," Seward had admitted.[12]

After the Civil War, however, Seward informed Napoleon III that the United States strongly disapproved of French interference in Mexico. In a show of force, Union General Philip Sheridan, with thirty thousand troops, was ordered to encamp along the Texas-Mexican border. Napoleon III quickly realized he could not afford to risk war with the United States. On April 5, 1866, the French government announced that its troops would leave Mexico completely within a year. By February 1867, the last French soldiers had boarded ships and begun their journey home.

Foolishly, Archduke Maximilian refused to surrender his throne and depart with the French Army. He chose instead to move his court from Mexico City north to the city of Queretaro. For several weeks, Maximilian and a few loyal troops held out against an army of nationalist Mexicans. But on May 14, 1867, Maximilian was forced to surrender. Quickly condemned to death by a Mexican military court, on June 19, 1867, Maximilian stood before a firing squad.

Dreams of a Canal

Seward had long wanted a canal to be built across Central America. Such a canal, connecting the Atlantic and Pacific oceans, would greatly aid American travel and commerce. In 1867, Seward concluded a treaty with Nicaragua granting the United States the right to construct a canal across that Central American country. Seward called it the "great American route."[13] The United States Senate ratified the Nicaraguan treaty in January 1868. Plans were made, but because of difficulty raising construction money, the canal was never built there.

Seward believed a canal across the Isthmus of Panama, which was controlled by the Colombian government, also might be possible. He tried to interest American millionaires Peter Cooper and William H. Vanderbilt in financing the project. American diplomat Caleb Cushing arranged a treaty permitting a United States company to construct a Panama canal. By April 1869, however, the Colombian government grew angry that no American money had yet been paid

and rejected the agreement. It would be thirty-five years before another treaty could be arranged and construction of a canal begun. The Panama Canal finally opened in 1914.

Building an American Empire

The Danish-owned Virgin Islands in the Caribbean Sea also attracted Seward's attention. He believed they would be useful as a United States naval base. Even before the end of the Civil War, he opened discussions with the Danish minister in Washington. Denmark was willing to sell, and President Johnson gave Seward permission to offer $5 million for the three islands of St. Thomas, St. John, and St. Croix. In December 1867, Seward submitted a treaty for the purchase of the islands at a cost of $7.5 million, but the Senate refused to act. When the United States

Midway Island

At Seward's urging, the United States Navy occupied little Midway Island in the Pacific Ocean in 1867. Located twelve hundred miles west of the Hawaiian Islands, the importance of Midway became obvious during World War II. In 1942, at the Battle of Midway, American planes sank four Japanese aircraft carriers. The victory marked the turning point of the war in the Pacific.

finally did purchase the three islands in 1917, it had to pay $25 million.

Buying Alaska

"Our population is destined to roll its resistless waves to the icy barriers of the North," Seward had declared in 1846.[14] In 1867, Seward and Russian Minister Edouard de Stoeckl finally came to terms. Not all Americans agreed that buying Alaska was a good idea. The *New York Herald* exclaimed that Alaska was "an ice house, a worthless desert with which to enable

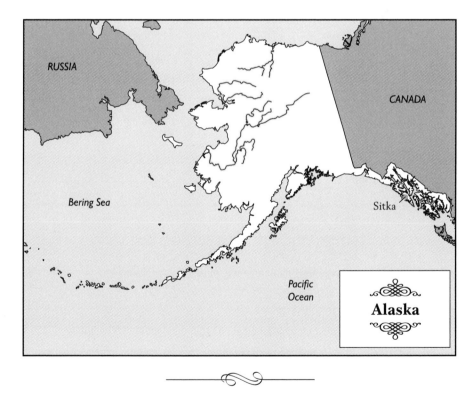

Seward believed the purchase of Alaska was his greatest accomplishment as secretary of state.

the Secretary of State to cover up . . . defeats he has suffered with the shipwrecked Southern policy of Andrew Johnson."[15] Seward, however, never lost faith. "Alaska," he insisted, "[will be] in the near future the great fishery, forest, and mineral storehouse of the world!"[16]

While Congress argued over the treaty, United States soldiers peacefully took possession of the region. On October 18, 1867, a company of United States soldiers stood at attention at the Russian fort at Sitka. In a formal ceremony, the Russian flag was lowered and the Stars and Stripes were raised. Cannons roared a salute, and Alaska became United States territory. The value of Alaska's vast natural resources would become apparent to Americans long before the territory became a state in 1959.

This engraving shows the Russian settlement at Sitka, Alaska. It was here that United States soldiers officially took possession of the Alaska Territory on October 18, 1867.

Impeachment

The Radical Republicans in Congress developed their own harsh Reconstruction plan, which they passed into law on February 20, 1867. The plan divided the South into five military districts. The Southern states were to remain under military control until elected legislatures had accepted the Fourteenth Amendment to the Constitution. This amendment granted all Americans, regardless of race, equal protection under the law. The Thirteenth Amendment, ratified in 1865, had already outlawed slavery.

The Radicals next sought to control President Johnson's Cabinet. The Tenure of Office Act, passed by Congress in February 1867, stated that people in certain government offices could not be removed by the president without Senate approval.

In time, Johnson decided to test that law because he believed it was unconstitutional. He demanded that Secretary of War Edwin Stanton resign. Stanton had been using his Cabinet position to promote Radical Republican views instead of Johnson's. As a result, on February 24, 1868, the House of Representatives voted 128 to 47 to impeach President Andrew Johnson for defying the Tenure of Office Act. Spectators silently sat in the Senate gallery on March 30, 1868, as the Senate grimly began the trial. Throughout the trial, Seward gave President Johnson his full support.

Senator Ben Wade of Ohio, the temporary president of the Senate, would become president if Johnson were removed. Radical Republicans sent word to Seward

that, if he would abandon Johnson, Wade would keep him on as secretary of state. "I'll see them damned first," snapped Seward. "The impeachment of the president is the impeachment of his cabinet."[17] He wrote to a friend that, if Johnson were convicted, "before the sun sets I shall retire from public life."[18]

The impeachment trial of Andrew Johnson lasted until May 16, 1868. At last, in the crucial vote, the Senate voted 35 for conviction and 19 for acquittal. Two thirds of the Senate, a total of thirty-six votes, had been needed to throw Johnson out of office. The president had survived by a single vote.

Man of the World

There is much gossip in relation to a projected marriage between Secretary Seward and a Miss Risley," noted Secretary of the Navy Gideon Welles in October 1868. "He is in his sixty-eighth year and she in her twenty-eighth."[1] Olive Risley was the attractive daughter of Hanson Risley, a Treasury Department employee. During 1868, Seward and Olive took frequent rides in his carriage and enjoyed country picnics. Lonely after the deaths of his wife and daughter, Seward found comfort in Olive Risley's company.

Last Official Duties

Snubbed by the Republican party, Andrew Johnson watched General Ulysses S. Grant win election as president in 1868. Bitterly, Johnson refused to take

any part in the inauguration ceremonies on March 4, 1869. Seward and other members of the Cabinet met that morning at the White House. Johnson sat busy at his desk until Seward suggested it was time to start for the inauguration. Johnson refused to budge. He kept the Cabinet busy at the White House until it was too late to attend the ceremonies. Although Seward was willing to forget past political differences and support Grant, Johnson remained stubborn to the end.

With the change of presidents, Seward resigned his office and prepared to leave Washington. "I never saw him," remarked a friend, "more happy than he is now; so different . . . from what he has been the last ten years."[2]

Seward's return to Auburn required much packing. More than a hundred boxes were shipped, containing furniture, papers, clothing, and mementos. In Auburn, Seward moved back into the old house on South Street with his son Will and Will's wife, Janet. "Mr. Lincoln's bust has gone to a place of honor in my library," Seward soon wrote to a friend. "We are well, and the robins are musically singing their greetings of the season."[3]

Seward at the age of sixty-eight was white-haired, bent, and weary. He walked slowly and somewhat unsteadily, and his right arm and hand showed signs of paralysis. He needed help to move around the house. To cure his ailments, he cheerfully told a friend he raised blisters on his hands by rowing on the lake, and he pushed a wheelbarrow while gardening in the yard. The chilly weather of Auburn bothered him, however,

Seward left Washington, D.C., in 1869 and retired to his home in Auburn, New York. Today, the Seward House is a museum open to the public.

and he was eager to see and do interesting things. More and more his thoughts turned to traveling.

To Alaska and Mexico

Seward chose to take a long retirement vacation in June 1869. He decided to visit Alaska and Mexico. He left Auburn on June 7 in a special railroad car, accompanied by Fred Seward and Fred's wife Anna, valet John Butler, and Auburn neighbor Abijah Fitch. The travelers journeyed from Rochester to Chicago, and on to Denver, Colorado, and Salt Lake City, Utah. Beyond the Missouri River, almost everything seemed new and

strange. The first transcontinental railroad had just opened in May 1869, making western travel easier. Seated in their luxury railroad car, they roared across the plains, past Indian camps and herds of buffalo.

After visiting San Francisco and Sacramento, California, the Seward party boarded a steamship and traveled north to Alaska. During the visit, Seward predicted that the territory would one day become a state in the Union. Returning to San Francisco, the travelers sailed next to Los Angeles. "The reception of William H. Seward in Southern California," declared the San Francisco *Examiner*, "has been made a perfect ovation everywhere in that beautiful country."[4]

From southern California, the tourists entered Mexico at Manzanillo, on the Gulf of California, early in October 1869. Mexicans remained grateful to Seward for helping rid that nation of French troops. The Mexicans decorated every town and city through which Seward passed with flags and banners. Joyful

Brigham Young
In Salt Lake City, Utah, Seward met Brigham Young, the famed leader of the Mormon Church. Young asked if it were true that Seward lived in the old Miller house in Auburn. When Seward said yes, Young revealed that, as a youthful carpenter in New York, he had built the fireplace mantel in Seward's front parlor.

Mexicans thronged the streets and welcomed him with shouts of praise. In Mexico City, Seward was the guest of Mexican President Benito Juarez.

From the city of Veracruz on the Gulf of Mexico, the travelers sailed across the Caribbean Sea. They spent three weeks in Havana, Cuba, and finally docked at Baltimore, Maryland, in February 1870. By March 12, Seward had reached home. His journeys had certainly tired him, but Seward happily insisted, "Travel improves health instead of exhausting it."[5]

Around the World

Olive Risley was eager to take a trip with Seward, and her father finally gave his consent. This time, Seward wanted to take a trip around the world. On August 9, 1870, Seward set out once more with his valet, and with Olive Risley, her sister Harriet, and their father. In San Francisco, they left Hanson Risley behind but were joined by California Governor Alexander W. Randall and his wife, as well as by Seward's nephew George Seward and his bride.

The long voyage across the Pacific Ocean carried the group to Japan. On January 9, 1871, Seward noted, "—In the five months since we left home, we reckon in distances made, eighteen thousand miles, an average of one hundred and twenty miles a day."[6]

In China, they spent two months exploring as far as the Great Wall. At Shanghai, China, Seward said farewell to the Randalls and the Sewards. George Seward was to begin duty as a United States diplomat there. This left Seward to travel alone with the two

young unmarried Risley women. He realized he needed to do something to make that arrangement appear completely respectable. For the sake of honor, Seward soon made arrangements for Olive Risley to become his legally adopted daughter.

Further Travels

From China, the Seward party journeyed onward through Southeast Asia and India. At Calcutta, India, the East India Railway Company provided Seward with a comfortable railroad car. He and the Risleys traveled north to within sight of the Himalaya Mountains. From Bombay, India, the tourists steamed across the Indian Ocean and through the recently opened Suez Canal to Egypt.

While in Egypt, Seward visited the Sphinx. "The Sphinx," he declared, ". . . is the most attractive of all the monuments. It is more than sixty feet high, its human head more than twelve feet long, the nose four feet long, the mouth two feet wide. . . . The Sphinx . . . excites the wonder of the beholder."[7]

The Holy Land (present-day Israel) was next on Seward's travel schedule. After a week in the city of Jerusalem, he and the Risleys traveled on to Greece. On June 25, 1871, they passed through the village of Tinos. "What a pretty, white village is this of Tinos," Seward remarked, "with the hills behind it terraced to their summits with orange-orchards and vineyards!"[8]

In Istanbul, Turkey, Seward enjoyed the greetings of the Turkish government. In Rome, the Pope granted him an audience. He and the Risleys reached Paris,

France, in August 1871. By that time, the journey was beginning to take a toll on Seward. He was gradually losing the use of both arms and now required the assistance of two servants. But he always remained in good spirits and was curious to see new sights.

Seward and his young companions finally arrived in New York City on October 2, 1871. A week later, they were back in Auburn. "When did a man of three score years and ten ever before go round the world?" one family friend said admiringly.[9] Seward estimated that he had traveled some forty-four thousand miles in the course of his fourteen-month trip. Later, he joked to friends, "I found that at my age, and in my condition of health, 'rest was rust'; and nothing remained, to prevent rust, but to keep in motion."[10]

Seward the Writer

Back in Auburn, Seward turned to writing. His friends had long urged him to write about his life. In October 1871, he began writing his autobiography. Each day, he dictated his memories to his son Fred or to a secretary.

After covering the first thirty-three years of his life, he decided to put aside the autobiography and instead write about his trip around the world. Olive Risley eagerly wanted to help. Together they devoted most of 1872 to writing the travel book. Based on both Olive's journal and Seward's own memories, they wrote 720 pages and included dozens of photographs. William H. Seward's *Travels Around the World*, describing the people and places he had visited, was published in 1873. It sold sixty thousand copies.

Death of a Statesman

Seward usually rose early and ate breakfast at around eight. Then he would turn to his mail and dictate his writing. He would often work through the morning, breaking only for a walk in the garden. Lunch at one o'clock was followed by a brief nap, most often on his couch in the study. In the afternoon, he welcomed visitors, wrote, or took a carriage ride or boat ride. Each evening after dinner he enjoyed playing cards.

But Seward was growing weaker. His arms had grown so weak he could eat only with the help of servants. Still, he always welcomed old friends to his home and had many long and interesting conversations. One visitor noted: "His head and heart were unchanged, but the poor limbs were all stricken. . . . He could not take our hands, nor even nod his head; but when we turned for one more good-bye look, he was still smiling, and so I ever picture him."[11]

On October 10, 1872, Seward rose as usual and worked through the morning at his desk. After lunch, he lay down on his couch but complained of difficulty breathing. The family sent for Dr. Theodore Dimon, the same man who had brought Seward the news when Lincoln was nominated for president in 1860. Dimon realized that Seward was failing rapidly. Sons Fred and Gus were notified by telegram to come. Late in the afternoon, Janet Seward asked her father-in-law if he had any final words for the family. Seward calmly whispered, "Love one another."[12] He died at four o'clock that afternoon.

During a lifetime of public service, William Seward never lost his faith in the greatness of the United States.

Within days, a solemn funeral procession carried the casket from the Seward home to Auburn's Fort Hill Cemetery. Seward was buried next to his wife, Frances, and his daughter, Fanny. Chiseled on his gravestone were the words he had long ago requested after his defense of William Freeman: "He was Faithful."

Seward left behind a legacy of greatness. As a United States senator, he had led the antislavery movement in the 1850s. During the Civil War, he had given President Lincoln tremendous support and guidance. As a diplomat, Seward helped keep Great Britain and France from aiding the Confederacy. Under President Andrew Johnson, he had the vision to purchase Alaska. There can be no doubt that William Seward loved the United States, and the record of his faithfulness will never be forgotten.

Chronology

1801—Born in Florida, New York, on May 16, the son of Dr. Samuel Seward and Mary Jennings Seward.

1816—Enters the sophomore class at Union College in Schenectady, New York.

1819—Runs away from college after a disagreement with his father; Briefly teaches at Union Academy in Eatonville, Georgia, but returns to Union College.

1820—Graduates with honors from Union College.

1822—Completes legal training at the New York City office of John Anthon; Passes the bar exam; Joins the Auburn, New York, law office of Judge Elijah Miller.

1824—Marries Frances Miller on October 20.

1828—Joins the Anti-Mason political movement.

1830—Elected to the New York state senate.

1833—Travels to Europe with his father.

1834—Joins the Whig political party; Runs for governor of New York and is defeated.

1835—Visits Virginia with his wife and son Frederick.

1838—Elected governor of New York.

1843—Returns to private law practice.

1846—Unsuccessfully defends African Americans Henry Wyatt and William Freeman in two murder trials.

1849—Elected United States senator.

1850—Argues against Clay's Compromise; Becomes a leading antislavery spokesman.

1854—Argues against the Kansas-Nebraska Act.

1858—Gives famous "Irrepressible Conflict" speech against slavery.

1859—Visits Europe for a second time.

1860—Defeated for the Republican nomination for president by Abraham Lincoln.

1861—Becomes United States secretary of state; The Civil War begins in April after the Confederate attack on Fort Sumter; His diplomatic efforts keep European nations neutral; Persuades President Lincoln to release Confederate diplomats during the *Trent* affair.

1862—Lincoln discusses Emancipation Proclamation with his Cabinet in July; Preliminary Emancipation Proclamation is issued in September after the Battle of Antietam; In December, Seward survives Republican senators' attempt to have him removed from the Cabinet.

1863—Using diplomacy, Seward prevents British-built warships from becoming part of the Confederate Navy; The Battle of Gettysburg, July 1–3, marks the turning point in the Civil War; Seward gives foreign diplomats a tour of New York.

1864—Abraham Lincoln elected to a second term as president in November.

1865—Attends Hampton Roads peace conference with Lincoln in February; The Confederates abandon Richmond, Virginia, on April 2; Seward suffers serious injuries in a carriage accident on April 5; Robert E. Lee surrenders his Confederate army to Ulysses S. Grant at Appomattox Court House, Virginia, on April 9; Lewis Paine attacks Seward at his home, and John Wilkes Booth assassinates Lincoln at Ford's Theatre on April 14; Frances Seward dies on June 21; Four assassination conspirators are hanged on July 7.

1866—Supports Reconstruction policies of President Andrew Johnson; Falls ill with cholera during "Swing Around the Circle" political tour; Daughter, Fanny, dies in October.

1867—Unsuccessfully negotiates to purchase Virgin Islands; Successfully makes the Alaska Purchase for $7.2 million.

1868—President Andrew Johnson survives impeachment trial.

1869 **–1870**—Seward retires to Auburn; Travels to Alaska and Mexico from June 1869 until March 1870.

1870 **–1871**—Travels around the world from August 1870 until October 1871.

1871—Begins writing autobiography.

1872—Writes *Travels Around the World* with Olive Risley; Dies on October 10 and is buried at Auburn's Fort Hill Cemetery.

CHAPTER NOTES

Chapter 1. Seward's Folly

1. John M. Taylor, *William Henry Seward* (New York: HarperCollins Publishers, 1991), p. 278.

2. Ibid., p. 123.

3. Frederick W. Seward, *Seward* (New York: Derby and Miller, 1891), vol. 3, p. 348.

4. Archie W. Shiels, *The Purchase of Alaska* (College: University of Alaska Press, 1967), p. 134.

5. Ibid., pp. 134–136.

6. Ibid., p. 137.

7. Ibid., p. 138.

8. Morgan B. Sherwood, ed., *Alaska and Its History* (Seattle: University of Washington Press, 1967), p. 277.

9. Glyndon G. Van Deusen, *William Henry Seward* (New York: Oxford University Press, 1967), p. 544.

10. Taylor, p. 281.

Chapter 2. The Lawyer From Auburn

1. Frederick W. Seward, *Seward* (New York: Derby and Miller, 1891), vol. 1, p. 20.

2. Thornton Kirkland Lothrop, *William Henry Seward* (Boston and New York: Houghton Mifflin Company, 1899), p. 2.

3. John M. Taylor, *William Henry Seward* (New York: HarperCollins Publishers, 1991), p. 12.

4. Seward, p. 22.

5. Taylor, p. 14.

6. Ibid., p. 16.

7. Frederic Bancroft, *The Life of William H. Seward* (Gloucester, Mass.: Peter Smith, 1967), vol. 1, pp. 38–39.

8. Taylor, p. 25.

9. Glyndon G. Van Deusen, *William Henry Seward* (New York: Oxford University Press, 1967), p. 27.

10. Bancroft, p. 55.

11. Van Deusen, p. 28.

12. Edward Everett Hale, Jr., *William H. Seward* (Philadelphia: George W. Jacobs & Company, 1910), p. 114.

13. Taylor, p. 38.

14. Van Deusen, p. 43.

15. Taylor, p. 42.

16. Van Deusen, p. 52.

Chapter 3. Governor of New York and Private Citizen

1. John M. Taylor, *William Henry Seward* (New York: HarperCollins Publishers, 1991), p. 42.

2. Frederic Bancroft, *The Life of William H. Seward* (Gloucester, Mass.: Peter Smith, 1967), vol. 1, p. 203.

3. Glyndon G. Van Deusen, *William Henry Seward* (New York: Oxford University Press, 1967), p. 55.

4. Taylor, p. 47.

5. Ibid., p. 48.

6. Ibid., p. 45.

7. Bancroft, p. 129.

8. Taylor, pp. 56–57.

9. Bancroft, p. 133.

10. Taylor, p. 58.

11. Bancroft, p. 183.

12. Taylor, p. 67.

13. Ibid., p. 68.

14. Edward Everett Hale, Jr., *William H. Seward* (Philadelphia: George W. Jacobs & Company, 1910), p. 208.

15. Taylor, p. 73.

16. Ibid.

17. Thornton Kirkland Lothrop, *William Henry Seward* (Boston and New York: Houghton Mifflin Company, 1899), pp. 50–51.

Chapter 4. Antislavery Senator

1. Glyndon G. Van Deusen, *William Henry Seward* (New York: Oxford University Press, 1967), p. 113.

2. John M. Taylor, *William Henry Seward* (New York: HarperCollins Publishers, 1991), p. 79.

3. Ibid., p. 84.

4. Frederic Bancroft, *The Life of William H. Seward* (Gloucester, Massachusetts: Peter Smith, 1967), vol. 1, pp. 246–249.

5. Van Deusen, p. 125.

6. Edward Everett Hale, Jr., *William H. Seward* (Philadelphia: George W. Jacobs & Company, 1910), p. 194.

7. Thornton Kirkland Lothrop, *William Henry Seward* (Boston and New York: Houghton Mifflin Company, 1899), p. 122.

8. Van Deusen, p. 152.

9. Hale, p. 218.

10. Bancroft, vol. 1, p. 362.

11. Ibid., p. 378.

12. Ibid., vol. 2, p. 83.

13. Taylor, p. 90.

14. Bancroft, vol. 2, p. 71.

15. Taylor, p. 107.

16. Carl Sandburg, *Abraham Lincoln: The Prairie Years* (New York: Harcourt, Brace & Company, 1926), vol. 2, p. 103.

17. Bancroft, vol. 1, p. 494.

18. Van Deusen, p. 211.

19. Bancroft, vol. 2, p. 77.

20. Van Deusen, p. 214.

21. Taylor, pp. 114–115.

Chapter 5. Presidential Candidate

1. Thornton Kirkland Lothrop, *William Henry Seward* (Boston and New York: Houghton Mifflin Company, 1899), pp. 195–196.

2. Glyndon G. Van Deusen, *William Henry Seward* (New York: Oxford University Press, 1967), p. 216.

3. John M. Taylor, *William Henry Seward* (New York: HarperCollins Publishers, 1991), p. 3.

4. Ibid., p. 5.

5. Frederic Bancroft, *The Life of William H. Seward* (Gloucester, Mass.: Peter Smith, 1967), vol. 1, p. 537.

6. Van Deusen, p. 224.

7. Carl Sandburg, *Abraham Lincoln: The Prairie Years* (New York: Harcourt, Brace and Company, 1926), vol. 2, p. 345.

8. Taylor, p. 8.

9. Van Deusen, p. 225.

10. Bancroft, vol. 1, p. 543.

11. Edward Everett Hale, Jr., *William H. Seward* (Philadelphia: George W. Jacobs & Company, 1910), p. 262.

12. Bancroft, vol. 1, p. 543.

13. Taylor, p. 121.

14. Van Deusen, p. 240.

15. Bancroft, vol. 2, pp. 38–39.

16. Taylor, p. 128.

17. Van Deusen, p. 246.

18. Bancroft, vol. 2, p. 38.

Chapter 6. A Nation Torn in Two

1. John M. Taylor, *William Henry Seward* (New York: HarperCollins Publishers, 1991), p. 138.

2. Frederic Bancroft, *The Life of William H. Seward* (Gloucester, Mass.: Peter Smith, 1967), vol. 2, p. 40.

3. Glyndon G. Van Deusen, *William Henry Seward* (New York: Oxford University Press, 1967), p. 253.

4. William Howard Russell, *My Diary North and South* (New York: Alfred A. Knopf, 1988), pp. 41–42.

5. Van Deusen, p. 279.

6. Ibid., p. 281.

7. Taylor, pp. 308–309.

8. Van Deusen, p. 283.

9. Taylor, p. 162.

10. Bancroft, vol. 2, p. 169.

11. Ibid., p. 176.

12. Van Deusen, p. 294.

13. Taylor, p. 174.

14. Van Deusen, p. 288.

15. Taylor, p. 169.

16. Bancroft, vol. 2, p. 261.

17. Ibid., p. 227.

18. Ibid., pp. 230–231.

19. Ibid., p. 234.

20. Ibid., p. 235.

21. Ibid., pp. 243–244.

22. Ibid., p. 244.

23. Taylor, p. 173.

24. Thornton Kirkland Lothrop, *William Henry Seward* (Boston and New York: Houghton Mifflin Company, 1899), p. 332.

25. Bancroft, vol. 2, p. 350.

26. Taylor, p. 201.

27. F. B. Carpenter, *The Inner Life of Abraham Lincoln: Six Months in the White House* (Lincoln: University of Nebraska Press, 1995), p. 22.

28. Van Deusen, p. 333.

29. Bancroft, vol. 2, p. 340.

30. Taylor, p. 205.

31. Ibid., p. 208.

32. Ibid.

33. Van Deusen, p. 347.

34. Taylor, p. 210.

Chapter 7. Lincoln's Right Hand

1. John M. Taylor, *William Henry Seward* (New York: HarperCollins Publishers, 1991), p. 212.

2. Frederic Bancroft, *The Life of William H. Seward* (Gloucester, Mass.: Peter Smith, 1967), vol. 2, p. 388.

3. Ibid., p. 389.

4. Taylor, p. 221.

5. Ibid., p. 234.

6. Glyndon G. Van Deusen, *William Henry Seward* (New York: Oxford University Press, 1967), p. 386.

7. Taylor, p. 241.

8. Van Deusen, p. 411.

9. Frederick W. Seward, *Seward* (New York: Derby and Miller, 1891), vol. 3, pp. 271–272.

Chapter 8. The Night of Horror

1. John M. Taylor, *William Henry Seward* (New York: HarperCollins Publishers, 1991), p. 240.

2. Frederick W. Seward, *Reminiscences of a War-Time Statesman and Diplomat 1830–1915* (New York: G. P. Putnam Sons, 1916), p. 259.

3. Taylor, p. 244.

4. Betty J. Ownsbey, Alias *"Paine": Lewis Thornton Powell the Mystery Man of the Lincoln Conspiracy* (Jefferson, N.C.: McFarland & Company, 1993), p. 101.

5. Taylor, p. 244.

6. Ibid.

7. Ibid., pp. 244–245.

8. F. B. Carpenter, *The Inner Life of Abraham Lincoln* (Lincoln: University of Nebraska Press, 1995), p. 291.

9. Taylor, p. 250.

10. Ibid.

11. Ibid.

12. Glyndon G. Van Deusen, *William Henry Seward* (New York: Oxford University Press, 1967), p. 434.

13. Noah Brooks, *Washington In Lincoln's Time* (New York: Rinehart & Company, 1958), p. 238.

14. Taylor, p. 248.

Chapter 9. Reconstruction

1. Glyndon G. Van Deusen, *William Henry Seward* (New York: Oxford University Press, 1967), p. 464.

2. Sculley Bradley, Richard Croom Beatty and E. Hudson Long, eds., *The American Tradition in Literature* (New York: W. W. Norton & Company, 1967), p. 1761.

3. John M. Taylor, *William Henry Seward* (New York: HarperCollins Publishers, 1991), p. 292.

4. Frederic Bancroft, *The Life of William H. Seward* (Gloucester, Mass.: Peter Smith, 1967), vol. 2, p. 448.

5. Taylor, p. 256.

6. Ibid., p. 260.

7. Ibid., p. 266.

8. Ibid., p. 267.

9. Ibid.

10. Ibid.

11. Ibid.

12. Bancroft, vol. 2, p. 425.

13. Taylor, p. 282.

14. Bancroft, vol. 2, p. 470.

15. Ernest Gruening, *The State of Alaska* (New York: Random House, 1968), p. 27.

16. William R. Hunt, *Alaska* (New York: W. W. Norton & Company, 1976), p. 178.

17. Taylor, p. 285.

18. Van Deusen, p. 481.

Chapter 10. Man of the World

1. John M. Taylor, *William Henry Seward* (New York: HarperCollins Publishers, 1991), p. 288.

2. Thornton Kirkland Lothrop, *William Henry Seward* (Boston and New York: Houghton Mifflin Company, 1899), p. 395.

3. Frederic Bancroft, *The Life of William H. Seward* (Gloucester, Mass.: Peter Smith, 1967), vol. 2, p. 516.

4. Taylor, p. 291.

5. Bancroft, vol. 2, p. 521.

6. William H. Seward, *Travels Around the World* (New York: D. Appleton and Company, 1873), p. 295.

7. Ibid., p. 541.

8. Ibid., p. 673.

9. Glyndon G. Van Deusen, *William Henry Seward* (New York: Oxford University Press, 1967), p. 561.

10. Bancroft, vol. 2, p. 524.

11. Ibid., pp. 525–526.

12. Taylor, p. 296.

Glossary

abolish—To do away with.

arsenal—An establishment for the manufacturing and storage of weapons and military equipment.

ballot—A sheet of paper used to cast a secret vote.

banish—To drive out or remove from a place.

bar exam—The test law students must pass before being allowed into the legal profession.

bounty—An extra allowance or reward.

collision—A clash or crash.

commerce—Buying and selling; business.

commissioner—A representative with governmental authority.

conviction—Belief.

custodian—One who guards; a keeper.

demoralize—To discourage or throw into disorder.

domestic—Of or relating to the home.

emancipation—Freedom for slaves or other oppressed people.

essential—Of the utmost importance.

generation—A group of individuals living during the same time period.

hemisphere—One half of the earth.

impeach—To accuse of or charge with a crime.

inevitable—Incapable of being avoided.

integrity—Honesty.

ironclad—Sheathed in iron armor.

irrepressible—Unstoppable.

isthmus—A narrow strip of land connecting two land areas.

malice—A desire to see another suffer.

manuscript—A piece of writing.

mementos—Souvenirs.

misdemeanor—A crime or misdeed.

ovation—A ceremony of greeting or thanks.

paralysis—The inability to move or function.

patent—The legal, exclusive right to manufacture a product.

pauper—A very poor person.

profound—Intense; deep.

radical—Desiring extreme change.

refinement—An improved or perfected condition.

render—To make.

rhetoric—The art of speaking or writing.

salvation—Deliverance from destruction or failure.

shackle—A binding or chain that confines the legs or arms.

successor—One who follows a person into an office or position.

tenant—Occupant; dweller.

tranquillity—A condition of calm or peace.

tuberculosis—A disease of the lungs caused by bacteria.

universal—Worldwide.

valet—A man's male servant.

FURTHER READING

Books

Bishop, Jim. *The Day Lincoln Was Shot*. New York: Harper & Row, Publishers, 1955.

Carpenter, F. B. *The Inner Life of Abraham Lincoln*. Lincoln and London: University of Nebraska Press, 1995.

Clark, Champ. *The Assassination—Death of a President*. Alexandria, Va.: Time-Life Books, Inc., 1987.

Fremon, David K. *The Alaska Purchase in American History*. Berkeley Heights, N.J.: Enslow Publishers, Inc., 1999.

Kent, Zachary. *Andrew Johnson*. Chicago: Children's Press, 1989.

———. *The Civil War: "A House Divided."* Hillside, N.J.: Enslow Publishers, Inc., 1994.

———. *The Story of the Election of Abraham Lincoln*. Chicago: Children's Press, 1986.

Ziff, Marsha. *Reconstruction Following the Civil War in American History*. Berkeley Heights, N.J.: Enslow Publishers, Inc., 1999.

Internet Addresses

"On the Irrepressible Conflict: William Henry Seward." *New York History Net*. n.d. <http://www.nyhistory.com/central/conflict.htm> (June 16, 2000).

"Seward's Folly." *Everything Alaska*. 1997–2000. <http://www.everythingalaska.com/eta.sfy.html> (June 16, 2000).

The William H. Seward House. n.d. <http://www.sewardhouse.org/> (June 16, 2000).

INDEX